The Secret

The Story of Brilliant, Beautiful, Handicapped Michael Jackson

by

Patricia Eddington

www.michaeljacksonthesecret.com

If I am wrong about this, please accept my apologies to all affected.

If I am right, God help us.

"humility, honor, poise, affection"

" wonderful person inside and out"
Beyonce

"A consummate gentleman"

"massively talented boy with a gentle soul"
Paul McCartney

Today someone said a negative remark about Michael Jackson. I said, "Michael Jackson was a good person." "How do you know?" was the reply. There was not time to explain. So began this book.

It was this statement that made me realize that no matter the cost to me, this book had to be written.

The statement below was in a book about Michael written by Bob Jones. It speaks of the chamber in Michael's room that was hidden in the closet. "There was a security lock system that was in the closet that opened a secret door." That secret room was shown by Maury Povich after Michael had died. Contrary to what was stated in the book the lock system was not that hidden. What was in that room was not stated in the Povich piece. The book did tell us. What was said was that the room was "packed with military-style costumes, children's toys and books. Beyond the door is a narrow carpeted stairwell lined with rag dolls descending into a secret chamber. It is a twisted version of a young child's bedroom. A bed is adorned with pillow cases imprinted with Peter Pan's face and the word "Neverland." Sitting on the bed is a Mickey Mouse telephone. On the wall are pictures of smiling diapered babies."

"Whatever may have happened to these boys probably happened here," the book said.

But I say, "All is not what it seems".

Contents

Chapter 1

The Vault at Gringotts

This is the story of a little boy who was surrounded by money, greed, selfishness, tremendous cruelty and more than anything horrible mistake, a little boy who swam with sharks that took bite after bite until there was not much left, a little boy who was bound by a secret even he did not know.

"My dress got caught and he was trying to help me," the dancer said. "Then I fell in the dirt and this icon was wiping me off." Michael Jackson was brushing the dirt off a dancer who had just fallen out of the car. [1] How Michael Jackson was that? I would come to find out that that was the beautiful being that was Michael Jackson, the beautiful being with a secret.

This was written for the real Michael Jackson. It is his gift. I am sorry it is so late. This is your gift, Michael, to clear your name and hopefully set you free.

11

I would not have written this if he wasn't being called the foulest of names. I would simply have written a letter to the family so they understood their son as I had and left it at that.

Writing this book frightens me. I could be stepping on some big powerful toes. I have stepped on toes before but none this powerful with so much money to lose. But right is right and wrong is wrong. What has happened here is so wrong, so egregious it borders on being an atrocity. Actually, it is an atrocity.

The funny thing is that, we loved Michael Jackson and I honestly believe that if we knew the truth we would have loved him and bought his music, anyway. Most of us loved or maybe just liked the little boy right from the start.

It started with the death of Michael Jackson. My friend told me. I always liked his music but I never went to his concerts and owned only one album. He was an entertainer and I had a life. I thought, and stated, that with all that had happened with him; to me he had died a long time ago. Actually, I had been a bit mad at the beautiful young man who somehow lost it all with foolish behavior.

As I was working on my computer with the television playing in the background I heard, in a testimony from someone who knew Michael Jackson very well, the words that would make me sob and be glued to my computer for days and months on end.

It was like the opening of the great vault at Gringotts in the Harry Potter movie, this big heavy vault, so well protected by steel and guards. Clang, clang, clang, I could picture big locks turning and turning. A vault kept locked by greed, money, confusion, betrayal, selfishness, denial, misunderstanding, and, yes, love and protection. Everything began to unlock. Everything made such sense. The big door was opened. The story was revealed right before my eyes. Michael was bizarre no more.

"No, how could this possibly be?" A wave of understanding and sadness flowed over me. What I had learned would not stop eating at me. My family had no clue why I would come to the family gathering only to have to go home because I forgot the salad or why I would forget the slightest thing I had just been told. I couldn't sleep. I would write incessantly in my bed, pull my car over to write what came to me as I drove and sometimes slept with the computer right next to me. It was exhausting. It was cathartic.

Once I realized what could be the real story of Michael Jackson, I researched everything I could find through buckets of tears. YouTube was my main source of information since I had to hear things for myself. I had to study the Michael Jackson I had hardly paid attention to for many years. I had to study the Michael Jackson not judged and misjudged by others. I had to be sure. What I learned would chill me to the core.

The pleading to be heard and defending without fighting, the bizarre looks, the bizarre life, the manikins, the chimp and the children, the Peter Pan obsession, the funny nicknames, the lack of money knowledge, the bedroom situation that got him in the mess that nearly cost him his life or maybe did, it all made perfect sense.

For those who will not or cannot change their minds about they think to be true concerning Michael Jackson there is nothing anyone can do. For those who want to see the icon and believe the fantasy there is nothing anyone can do. But for those who are willing to let go of the icon, to see his humanity and really understand Michael Jackson as he is, come with me.

Chapter 2

Not Childhood

Michael always thought his problems were due to fact that he didn't have a normal childhood or any childhood at all. This is the song he wrote about his feelings concerning his childhood.[2] Please read it closely. It will matter later.

"Childhood"

Have you seen my Childhood?
I'm searching for the world that I come from
'Cause I've been looking around
In the lost and found of my heart...

No one understands me
They view it as such strange eccentricities...
'Cause I keep kidding around
Like a child, but pardon me...

People say I'm not okay
'Cause I love such elementary things...
It's been my fate to compensate,
for the Childhood

I've never known...

Have you seen my Childhood?
I'm searching for that wonder in my youth
Like pirates in adventurous dreams,
Of conquest and kings on the throne...

Before you judge me, try hard to love me,
Look within your heart then ask,
Have you seen my Childhood?

People say I'm strange that way
'Cause I love such elementary things,
It's been my fate to compensate,
for the Childhood I've never known...

Have you seen my Childhood?
I'm searching for that wonder in my youth
Like fantastical stories to share
The dreams I would dare, watch me fly...

Before you judge me, try hard to love me.
The painful youth I've had

Have you seen my Childhood...

This is amazingly the story of Michael Jackson. He was always searching for the answer to why he was so different. His belief was that he was different because he lost his childhood and was trying to get it back. I don't agree with him. I believe there was a different reason.

Michael embraced those who were like him in his lost childhood. Those people included Brooke Shields and Elizabeth Taylor. They afforded him some comfort and were somewhat like him but they were certainly not entirely like him. They did not have "strange eccentricities". People didn't label them "childlike" and they did not own manikins, bring chimps to tea parties, nor did they cry all the time.

Michael also visited Shirley Temple Black, a child star of the 1930s who also spent her childhood on stage. They had phone conversations and shared wonderful times together. She was a lot like him in their childhood situations. She too had to dance and practice during her childhood years and missed out on a lot. But again, she became a US ambassador to Ghana. Her life, though starting out like Michael's, took a much different path.

The largest glitch in Michael's thinking that the loss of his childhood was the reason for his being unusual was his brother, Marlon.

Marlon lived virtually the same life as Michael. Except for being just one year older he was with him for every show, was beaten according to Michael more than Michael, was made to perform all night and go to school the next day. He lost the same amount of childhood as Michael. But today, Marlon is a successful person. Marlon stayed married to the same wife all of his life. Marlon used the Jackson 5 money to go into real estate. Marlon owns businesses. Marlon is a normal and successful adult though he had the same childhood as Michael.

Some people thought Michael to be eccentric. Some thought him to be simply crazy. Some thought his entrapment and subsequent sadness was due to his celebrity status. It is true that celebrity is a cage you would not want to live in but it does not cause you to hang around with chimps and manikins.

So, what is the answer that eluded Michael all of his life? What is the secret?

Maybe this poem from years ago will help you understand. I shortened it for you but it basically goes like this:

There's a hole in the bucket, dear Liza...
There's a hole.
Then fix it dear Henry...
With what should I fix it, dear Liza, with what?
With a straw, dear Henry.
The straw is too long, dear Liza, too long.
Then cut it dear Henry, dear Henry, cut it!
With what shall I cut it, dear Liza, with what?
With an ax, dear Henry, an ax.
The ax is too dull, dear Liza, too dull.
Then sharpen it dear Henry, sharpen it!
With what should I sharpen, dear Liza, with what?
With a stone, dear Henry, a stone.
The stone is too dry, dear Liza, too dry.
Then wet it dear Henry, dear Henry, wet it.
With what should I wet it, dear Liza, with what?
With water, dear Henry, with water.
But how shall I get it? Dear Liza, with what?
In the bucket, dear Henry, dear Henry, in the bucket.
But there's a hole in the bucket. Dear Liza, there's a hole.

None of the books I have read had given a reason for the situation with Michael.

You see, there's a hole in the bucket. I am just sorry I never got the chance to tell Michael what it was. He would have been able to deal with it if he knew what the problem was. He would have been happy. He would have been fine.

At least I can tell you.

Chapter 3

The Difference

This book does not disparage Michael Jackson. In fact, though I was originally a fan, I began to really love Michael Jackson that day sitting at my computer and through my experience writing this book.

From the book "The Man Behind the Mask": "One thing is certain. Michael will not be forgotten. But will he be remembered as a misunderstood unfairly maligned legend, or a monstrous, self-hating, mentally ill deviant?" [3]

Maybe there is another choice.

Anyone who knew Michael Jackson, whether in real life or from the media, can picture the difference in him as opposed to the regular guy next door. Let's suppose that Michael Jackson was just an everyday guy who happened to be so talented that he was renown throughout the world. Let's just say that except for his profound talent and great marketing by professionals he was the guy next door. Picture that for just this exercise. Look at a regular guy that is nearby. Look at the men surrounding you. Or, you can picture others in the entertainment business who are very successful. Picture Robin Williams who is as talented as Michael in his own domain. Maybe picture Michael

Jordan who is as talented as Michael in his domain. Picture maybe, Robert De niro or Al Pacino who are as talented as Michael in their own domains. How is Michael different from Robin Williams, Michael Jordan, Robert De niro, Al Pacino?

We have become accustomed to the odd behavior of Michael Jackson but to understand the reality of what I am about to tell you it is important to see the actual, in your face, difference.

Compare Michael to another successful adult in show business and the gap will appear and a huge gap it will be. Read each of these and think of an adult you know of and compare the action of Michael to that person.

Michael Jackson as an adult:

*Questioned by fans if had sex

*Had hundreds of children sleep in his bed

*Cried all the time

*Lonely all the time

*Blew kisses

*Covered his mouth a lot in public

*Hung out with children

*Played water balloons with Macaulay Culkin

*Often pleaded for understanding

*Had no concept of money

*Wore pajamas to court

* Needed children to sleep in his bed

*Build Neverland as home

*Nicknamed friend babyish name"

*Made up club called Apple Head Club

*Held his kid tightly over balcony for people to see

*Couldn't understand why it was wrong for children to sleep in his bed

*Said after being burnt, "I liked riding in the ambulance. It was wild with the sirens wailing"

*Waved to the audience after severely burned

*Was best friends are young kids and motherly older lady

*Was asked in an interview if he had sex after his marriage without being annoyed

*Waved to paparazzi after speaking badly of them

*Lived with parents until 27

*Stated he was still a boy at age 27

*At age 45 would say, "That's not nice, right?"

*Assigned someone to care for kids after death without telling her

*Had to have manikins in his room

*Had Bubbles the Chimp for a best friend

*Had children for best friends

* Had three hour phone calls to a child

*Talked about cartoons on phone

*Nicknamed "Applehead" throughout his whole life

*Brought his chimp to a formal tea party

*Told a person in labor not to curse but to say "shoot" and "fudge"

*Personally owns statues of Mickey Mouse and Pinocchio

*Walked into court holding his mother's hand

*Stated, "I always want to play hide and seek.'

*Stated on camera, "I cry an awful lot."

*Stated, "I could heal Hitler"

*Held hands with Brooke Shields at the Grammys but kissed Emmanuel Lewis on the cheek [4]

*Stated as an adult, "I have to play"

* Stated about a child, as a 30 year old "That's Emmanuel Lewis one of my best friends."

*I'm the one who looks stinky." Bashir tape [5]

*Stated, "I walked around holding these baby dolls and I'd be crying"

*Called a business associate "very, very, devilish". As he held up posters of him with horns [6]

*Owned a Mr. Toad golf cart

*On still living home at 24: "It was the height of Thriller. I thought I was still a little kid. I'm still a boy. It's not time for me to leave home yet"

*Stated "When people make up stories that I don't want to be who I am, it hurts me."

*Told this story on the Bashir tape, "Prince said, "He has a stomach which looks like a balloon". I said, "Prince, You are right. But if you see him don't say it in front of him because you could make him cry". [7]

*Stated on camera, "Most people don't call me by my name Michael either Applehead or another name which I won't say. It's not a bad word." [8]

*Had this keepsake: "To Apple Head. Always remember keep Apple Head Club Doo Doo Head Alive.'" The photograph was signed by Macaulay Culkin who added 'Doo Doo Head' after his name. This was on a card on Michael's nightstand. The Apple Head Club was a secret society Michael encouraged his young friends to join.

* Had a secret room in his house with a bed with Peter Pan sheets and ragdolls.

And the list goes on…

"When we were together we were two little kids having fun." Brook Shields

"I know you're still a child…" Jermaine Jackson, "Word to the Badd"

"In some ways, he was like a child, and a very sweet and gentle child, and he wanted me to tell him many, many stories, stories about the chimpanzees, the forests, animals, anything. He told me he liked the way I told stories." Jane Goodall

a fawn

Sensitive

Childlike

Gentle

"among the sweetest and most talented people"

Childlike, sensitive, loving, caring

"fawn in a burning forest" Steven Speilberg

Just a child

"Extremely sensitive, very gentle, very childlike" Attorney Tom Mesereau

"Jackson was pure and childlike." Deepak Chopra

Fragile

In the Bashir tapes you can see Michael telling about his abuse. For us it was not as bad since he was now an adult who should have grown to be able to handle it. Like many adults who, though they are scarred but are survivors and they know it was in the past. But for Michael it was not in the past.

When you look at the tapes you will see Michael put his hand to his face. He does it quickly and with an open hand. If you have children or work with them you will have seen this gesture before. It surely shows a child's gesture. It later changes to a more adult gesture with fingers closed and over the eyes. Keep that in mind when you read on in this book.

Picture this contrast. It is important that you see the difference. There is undoubtedly, obviously, something severely wrong. I can tell you what it is.

Chapter 4

The Secret

"I cry often because it hurts. It hurts to be me".   Michael Jackson

"Everything is foreign to me or new." Michael Jackson

"I was raised on stage. I am happy on stage. I could sleep on stage. When I'm off it is another story. It's hard to relate to people in everyday life." Michael Jackson"

"But don't forget this is the weirdest man on the planet." Bob Jones
(9)
The mystery concerning Michael Jackson was his ability to be so in control and so broken at the same time.

I am asking you to open your minds and love or at least understand Michael Jackson -- not the icon or the fantasy but the real person. Love or simply accept Michael Jackson the way he would have loved or accepted you.

I can tell you why Michael was a tortured soul. I can tell you why he was so lonely. I can tell you about the "hole in the bucket". You have to open your mind to accept it.

I can tell you this will not be easy. I had a hard time believing it myself. I can tell you that you will bounce from "Can this be possible?" to "No, way" to "Oh, my God". I know because with my almost 50 years of experience in this field, I bounced too.

The infamous words that I heard sitting at my computer that fateful day, fateful for me anyway, were "Donald Duck". Michael was watching Donald Duck on his computer as I found out he so often did. He often spoke to children for hours about cartoons and Paul McCartney said that Michael Jackson could sit and watch cartoons all day. Those were the words that showed me what I believe to be the truth about Michael Jackson. Michael Jackson was all of his adult life, a handicapped child.

I will show you here that Michael Jackson, for all intents and purposes, all of his life fluctuated between five and ten years old because of left brain impairment and lack of proper teaching being generally in daily life an eight year old boy. Yes. Michael Jackson was eight years old.

I believe that Michael was left brain impaired and, though many school districts vary on their terminology, where I worked Michael would have been labeled TBI which is short for Traumatic Brain Injury.

I believe that Michael was not only left brain impaired but also right brain brilliant.

You need a brief lesson on the workings of the brain to understand how this is possible. The two hemispheres of the brain are called the right brain and left brain. They work both together and separately. Most of the day in daily life a person is using the right brain or memory. The left brain only works when needed to figure things out that were not already learned and then the lessons learned are placed in the right brain or in memory to be used unconsciously throughout the day. Driving in daily life is right brain or memory but entering a freeway is left brain as is parallel parking. Michael could do neither entering a freeway or parallel parking. He could drive, however.

The left brain deals with logical thinking, analysis and accuracy. A mathematician is a good example of a left brain dominant person. The right brain deals with creativity, feeling and aesthetics, beauty, art, graphics and that which is attractive.

Let's start with right brain information. I say that Michael was right brain brilliant for three reasons. Michael by nature had what it took to be creative. It showed at such a very young age and was why his father Joseph kept saying, "Do it like Michael, do it like Michael". Michael was unbelievably talented even at a very young age. The second reason was the fact that he knew something was wrong and was always searching for the place where he belonged. This searching showed higher right brain functioning and is what caused him to continue to say how lonely he was all of his life. The third reason and the real indication to me that Michael was extraordinary in his right brain abilities was his profound and absolutely beautiful poetry.

Had there not been a left brain impairment there is no telling how far he would have gone. He would have been Michael Jackson the great entertainer normal guy who would have been able to get all he needed from life the same way as the rest of us. Michael was so left brain impaired that he was handicapped, he was developmentally handicapped.

I will try to explain this as best I can. This is a bit intricate so you may have to read it a few times to understand. I hope you give it the time to do so.

The right brain deals with art, creativity, music, dance, storytelling, love, personality, fun, cleverness, etc. Does that sound like Michael? Michael was brilliant and very active with all things right brained and it was the right brain person that we saw as the audience in his videos, music, dancing, singing and interviews with his interviews being mostly storytelling. The left brain, along with other things, deals with logic and logic is where all of his problems existed.

Logic was Michael's entire problem.

In his first interview with Oprah, you can see the right brain Michael telling a story of his life to her with ease. He was completely in control. When Elizabeth Taylor entered the scene you see Elizabeth sitting in a chair and Michael standing behind her. You can see here that Michael is completely disengaged as Oprah and Elizabeth talk. He is staring blankly into space instead of joining their conversation as we would (But then we wouldn't have needed Elizabeth in the first place). Oprah said later that when looking back they didn't even offer him a chair. Michael spoke to Oprah using his very capable right brain abilities but at that moment when Elizabeth came in he was out of his element and he needed left brain logic to figure out what to do with himself. That logic was not there for him to use so he disengaged. [10]

Maturity:

The left brain is used every day to teach us all things logical and there are hundreds or thousands or tens of thousands or perhaps hundreds of thousands of tiny lessons we learn through logic every day. We don't know how many there are nor do we understand how minute they are but each of those lessons builds us into the logical adult we become.

The logical part of the brain is the part that deals with maturity. Growing as an adult depends on "logical learning". That logical learning, which professionals call "residual learning", is learning that takes place in tiny increments and builds us tiny bit by tiny bit every day.

Each lesson learned builds us into an adult just like someone would build a skyscraper brick by brick. If the delivery of those bricks to build the skyscraper was very slow or not at all at times, the skyscraper would end up being only a small building or not being build at all. Those lessons build us little by little into adults and the lack of those lessons will leave us a child.

Without that logical learning of each day Michael did not mature as much as he should have. Michael was known for his practical jokes and was often called a child. He would throw pie at his coworkers, throw water balloons at fans and, of course, there was Neverland. Growing depends on that logical learning that takes place every day without our knowledge that Michael did not get not only because of his disability but because he was not in the proper environment to learn.

You can teach a person lessons they should have learned through their left brain which they can place in memory or place in the right brain. So they do grow but the lessons are too numerous to ever bring the person to equality with someone not left brain impaired. Michael, being so isolated from children for reasons I will explain later, would have always been from five to ten years old generally in daily life around eight years old, which was why he needed to hang around with children.

As I said before, things can be taught that are left brain things and remembered using right brain or memory and that did happen with Michael. This added to the confusion because the people saw his brilliant right brain creations that were peppered with a bit of logic from memory and often a lot of logic from others and thought him an undamaged adult.

Those who helped Michael with whatever he was doing added logic to it inadvertently to make whatever the project was better just as Berry Gordy told Michael to say, "just look over your shoulder, Honey" to make "I'll Be There" such a great song. People, without realizing it, added just a bit of logic to his work and made it great and make his situation even more confusing to the average person trying to figure out Michael Jackson.

Imagine what would have been if Michael had left brain ability to add to his own work. What amazing art we would have had.

What you acquire from lessons learned unconsciously every day through logical learning would bring us to maturity. The lack of or the lessening of those lessons and God awful celebrity left Michael lost and fighting to be understood and understand. It left him a lost eight year old boy. His right brain being so strong fought for the missing piece to the story while the left brain kept it from him.

Michael was not your typical left brain impaired person. The reason for that is that he was so right brain brilliant. It is this unusual situation, this unusual combination that caused the general population including many professionals to misunderstand and misjudge him. Their assumption that he was "normal" from the start, caused them to go in completely the wrong direction. After all, he was a celebrity multimillionaire who had so many successful accomplishments. He was the King of Pop, a songwriter, a music writer, a businessman, a successful adult. Leaning on the assumption that he was all of those things and trying to make sense from there, made the normal adult in his life assume what was not true.

Macaulay Culkin said in an interview with Larry King that Michael had a hard time communicating what he was trying to say. To those who had seen him in interviews it seems he could communicate just fine. What you really saw was storytelling peppered a bit with some logic that had been fed to him throughout his life that he had in his memory.

When the Handlers or Gatekeepers, who you will learn about later, would be worried about what he would say that could get him in trouble, they would coach him so what you saw was practiced or out and out choreographed speech.

32

Over and over again I would read of people asking Michael a question only to have the person answer the question or elaborate on it. At that time the logical response given by the other person became Michael's information, his possession.

To make matters even worse, Michael had a great memory. Michael had an amazing memory. "Michael could remember the choreographer's direction immediately and execute the step with precision, Diana (Ross) would have to rehearse for hours and would still have some trouble with it" [11]

Any logical concept that he was taught in an instance became a learned thing for Michael and it was stored either in memory or as a right brain usable concept. Now it was his. Paul McCartney once said, "Michael would pick your brain."

On his shyness: If you were left brain impaired and the world was constantly asking you to communicate with what would come from your left brain would you be confident? Wouldn't you be continually afraid that you would be asked questions you could not answer or put in positions in which you could not cope? Did you know that Michael would throw up before every interview? Now you know why.

If you are put in the position to have to communicate by using your left brain abilities and you have few left brain abilities you would have to figure out what to do but you would have to figure out what to do using your left brain. It takes a logical left brain to tell why the left brain couldn't communicate! Quite the catch 22.

Comparison to others:

I thought I would give you an example of the difference between right brain and left brain using actual people whose personalities would help you understand. I am going to try to give you an idea of the situation concerning right brain and left brain.

These people are not impaired. They are however right or left brain dominant. Using these examples will hopefully give you an understanding of the situation with Michael. I am going to do this using real people that you know or know of. Remember, these people are not damaged or impaired. They are simply right or left brain dominant.

Let's show the contrast between very right brained Robin Williams and very left brained Albert Einstein. Quite the contrast and that is the point. Could you picture Robin Williams sitting in a class listening to or figuring out the theory of relativity? Not that he couldn't learn such a concept, but it would be hard to imagine him interested. Robin Williams is very right brain dominant. He could learn it but would not be enthralled for sure.

Then take Albert Einstein. Could you picture putting him on stage and saying, "Come up with 5 funny things and act them out"? Would he look foolish standing there? Probably. Would he look like he had something wrong with him? Probably. Would he be at a total loss for words? Unless it pertained to what he already knew I believe, yes. And again, this is a person who is not impaired. I am not saying that Albert Einstein could not tell a joke. I am a fan of his and have read his jokes. I am saying that his talent extraordinaire was in the realm of all that is part of the left brain.

Now what about Michael Jackson? He was as talented in his expertise as Robin Williams or Albert Einstein were in theirs. With Michael the handlers and experts and the groomers helped but without that talent, they would have had nothing to work with. Without that talent that was Michael Jackson's alone, all would have fallen by the wayside.

When I was in college we had a lecturer at my university. The lecturer had come in late and seemed like he had just been dragged out of bed. I decided to make a bathroom trip in the middle of his speech which I think was more celebrated because of who he was than what he was saying.

The bathroom of the psychiatry unit of the University where our meeting was held taught me more than the famous lecturer whose name escapes me. The walls were covered in writing and not the kind you find at Burger King. These were people seeking help any way they could, just like Michael was always asking people for help. One such question which seemed to be on the wall for quite a while, stuck with me because I had the answer and was not able to reach the person who needed it. The reason I am mentioning it here is because it shows two things. One is that Michael was not the only person with situations that separated the left brain and the right brain. But more importantly it showed that the left brain dealt with the "head" while the right brain dealt with the "heart". Remember Michael always spoke of love.

Here is the question:

"My head is in a guillotine, the blade comes down. My head is on one sided, my body on the other. Which side will I be on?"

Do you have the answer? The answer is "both" and "neither". Just as your body cannot live without both your brain and your heart so can you not live without a connection between your left brain and your right brain. A person without a right brain would be robotic. A person without a left brain would be vegetative.

One question you may have is whether you can see impairment? The answer is "no". Many of the students I worked with had no visible damage that could be seen on an MRI or any other medical or mechanical scan. The impairment was obviously there and showed through testing and actions but most often did not show up on any physical testing. Therefore, I am using the word impaired instead of damaged because damage can be seen on medical machines. Impairment in this context makes the area simply not work.

This may help:

Once a person close to me had a car accident where he landed on his head on the pavement and broke his neck. He was a completely different person after the accident and I had a hard time looking in his face and acknowledging the person before me was not the person I had known. I had to find a way to cope with it so I told myself to see him as a twin and the other twin had died. It worked well for me.

With Michael there was no death but two completely different renderings of the same person. You would probably be best off if each time you saw him you deciphered whether you were seeing right brain Michael or left brain Michael. That might help.

The two sides of Michael Jackson:

I am going to give you one example of the two sides of Michael Jackson. The poem is the adult side, the right brain brilliant side of Michael that lead everyone astray including Michael. This was written by Michael and is the beautiful compilation of words making a "story".

The other example showing left brain Michael was what happened once before Michael was to go on stage in rehearsals.

Right Brain Michael:

Magical Child - Part 1

Once there was a child and he was free
Deep inside he felt the laughter
The mirth and play of nature's glee
He was not troubled by thoughts of hereafter
Beauty, love was all he'd see

He knew his power was the power of God
He was so sure, they considered him odd
This power of innocence, of compassion, of light
Threatened the priests and created a fright
In endless ways they sought to dismantle
This mysterious force which they could not handle

In endless ways they tried to destroy
His simple trust, his boundless joy
His invincible armor was a shield of bliss
Nothing could touch it, no venom, no hiss
The child remained in a state of grace
He wasn't confined in time or place
In Technicolor dreams, he frolicked and played
While acting his part, in Eternity he stayed

Soothsayers came and fortunes were told
Some were vehement, others were bold
In denouncing this child, this perplexing creature
With the rest of the world he shared no feature
Is he real? He is so strange
His unpredictable nature knows no range
He puzzles us so, is he straight?
What's his destiny? What's his fate?

And while they whispered and conspired
Through endless rumors to get him tired
To kill his wonder, trample him near
Burn his courage, fuel his fear
The child remained just simple, sincere

All he wanted was the mountain high
Color the clouds, paint the sky
Beyond these boundaries, he wanted to fly
In nature's scheme, never to die

Don't stop this child, he's the father of man
Don't cross his way, he's part of the plan
I am that child, but so are you
You've just forgotten, just lost the clue

Inside your heart sits a Seer
Between his thoughts; he can hear
A melody simple but wondrously clear
The music of life, so precious, so dear

If you could for one moment know
This spark of creation, this exquisite glow
You would come and dance with me
Kindle this fire so we could see
All the children of the Earth
Weave their magic and give new birth
To a world of freedom with no pain
A world of joy, much more sane

Deep inside, you know it's true
Just find that child, it's hiding in you. (12)

Left Brain Michael:

In 1984, when filming a commercial Michael went to the bathroom. While there he let out an ungodly scream. They all rushed in to find that Michael dropped his rhinestone glove in the toilet. Bob Gerardi said trying not to laugh, "Ok somebody get a hanger or something." With that Michael said, "Oh, forget it" and fished it out. Then he said, "Anyone got a hair dryer?"

Here is what really happened. Right brain brilliant Michael was doing his normal right brain performing when he went to the bathroom, dropped his glove in the toilet and was trapped. Why couldn't he just fish it out himself? Because to figure out that he could do so required left brain thinking and he didn't have it. When Bob said they could just fish it out Michael realized the "story" of what could be done to get the glove and it became a right brain concept and he fished it out himself, which is what we would have done from the beginning.

So, why did Michael relate so well to the character of Peter Pan? In reality there is no Peter Pan but there are adults who stay children due to whatever occurred in their lives. Michael was one of them. Michael Jackson was not Peter Pan in his heart, as he believed. Michael was Peter Pan in his head.

Chapter 5

The Tragedy

As I went through the literature on Michael it was very hard to imagine the Michael I had seen on album covers and so in control on stage was disabled. I had to continually remind myself of two things. One was Donald Duck along with the statement of the juror from his 2003 trial who said, "We felt Michael was still a kid in a man's body".[13] The other thing was "The Handlers". I will explain about them later. I had to keep those two things in my mind at all times to sift through the garbage and bring this concept to light.

Apply the concept that Michael was really eight years old and you will see all questions answered.

I worked with many students of various disabilities from minor to severe to profound. Sometimes there was a history of maybe an accident or a situation prior to birth. Never in my career had I heard so many stories that could have brought about such an injury than I had heard from Michael Jackson. I don't know what caused his situation but here are some of the stories concerning Joe Jackson.

"He would throw us against the wall as hard as he could." Michael Jackson

"He would throw you and hit you as hard as he can. "Joe. No, you're going to kill him. No! No! Joe, it's too much" He would be breaking furniture." Michael Jackson (14)

In one altercation recalled by Marlon, Joseph held Michael upside down by one leg and "pummeled him over and over again with his hand, hitting him on his back and buttocks".(15) Today it was announced on the television that the partial autopsy results stated that Michael had arthritis in his lower spine.

Joseph would also trip or push his sons into walls. "One night while Michael was asleep, Joseph climbed into his room through the bedroom window, wearing a fright mask and screaming. He said he wanted to teach the children not to leave the window open when they went to sleep. For years afterward, Jackson said he suffered nightmares about being kidnapped from his bedroom. Joseph acknowledged in 2003 that he regularly whipped Jackson as a child." (16)

"Joseph once locked Michael in the closet for hours," said a friend of the Jackson Family. "That was traumatizing, horrible for him." (17)

When Michael was five, he toddled into a room and had his breath taken away when Joseph tripped him and he fell to the ground bloodied. "That's for whatcha' did yesterday," Joseph said, "And tomorrow I'm gonna get you for what you're gonna do today." From that point onward, whenever young Michael walked into a room he looked left, then right, when entering a room as if crossing the street. (18)

For many years after that Michael and Marlon suffered vivid nightmares of being kidnapped in the night. (19)

Once when Michael was late to rehearsal, Joseph came up from behind and shoved him into a stack of musical instruments.(20)

"It was Do it like Michael." He practiced us with a belt in his hand and if you missed a step expect to be…(shows whipping gesture). He would tear you up if you missed. We were nervous because if you didn't do it the right way he would tear you up, really get you. I got it a lot of times but I think my brother Marlon got it the worst because he had a hard time at first and he tried so hard. (Michael's way of saying it was so sympathetic here) It was always "Do it like Michael, do it like Michael". Michael Jackson

"How often would he beat you?" Martin Bashir asked Michael.

"Too much."

Bashir: "Would he only use a belt?" (Michael begins to cry here)

"Why do you do this to me? No more than a belt."

"What else would he use to hit you with?"

"Iron cords, whatever's around. Throw you up against the wall as hard as he could. See, it's one thing to…"

Bashir: "but you were only a child, you were a baby."

"I know, I would remember hearing our mother scream, "Joe, you're going to kill him. Stop it, you're gonna kill him. I was so fast he couldn't catch me half the time but when he could catch me, Oh, my God. It was bad. It was really bad." [21]

So was the problem with Michael caused by getting thrown against the wall repeatedly by a large man when he was five years old?

I don't know since I had never had a student who was thrown against a wall repeatedly since he was five years old.

Was Michael's problem caused by being held upside down and pummeled over and over again since he was five years old?

I don't know. I had never had a student who was pummeled over and over since he was five years old. In fact, I don't think I had ever had a student who was pummeled at all.

And how long does it take to pummel a child over and over? How long was Michael held upside down to be pummeled over and over?

How long can a five year old be hung upside down with his heart racing from fear without being damaged?

I don't know. I have never had a student hung upside down involuntarily, unable to get up when he needed to get up and pummeled at the same time.

Was Michael's problem caused by the fact that a child who is in Kindergarten or First Grade had to work until 3 or 4 in the morning and then get up for school? By the way, I wonder if he was allowed to bring his blankie? Just a thought.

Could that have caused an injury? I don't know. Could it cause insomnia for a lifetime...very possibly.

As I see on the television Michael Jackson working with Lou Ferrigno, I wonder if the comparison of him to young Michael and Joe

Jackson would be accurate. If Lou Ferrigno would suddenly with all his might pick up Michael and throw him against the wall as hard as he could would it compare to Joe Jackson throwing Michael, five year old Michael, against the wall as hard as he could as Michael said he had done?

Please picture that image in your mind. Picture a grown man who was a steel worker picking up a five year old and tossing him against the wall "as hard as he could". Picture what you would do if you saw that today. Imagine it happening right before your eyes. Please take the time to imagine it. Then imagine it being your child. Imagine your five year old being tossed against the wall by an adult. What fear would go through your mind? What damage would you fear happened to that child? Would you think to call an ambulance even if the child seemed fine?

So what happened? Did being thrown into a wall too many times, being hung upside down and pummeled or woken up at the age of 5 each night to perform until 3 or 4 in the morning then try to go to KINDERGARTEN the next day cause damage? Who really knows and again how long can you hang a five year old upside down before damage is done? We do know there was something wrong.

Ask yourself this…

Would an adult wear pajamas to court? No
Would a sick eight year old boy? Yes

Would an adult consider another eight year old to be his best friend? No
Would an eight year old? Yes

Would an adult be nicknamed Applehead head? No
Would an eight year old? Yes

Would an adult make up "The Applehead Club? No
Would an eight year old? Yes

Would an adult have sleepovers with young boys? No
Would an eight year old? Yes

Would an adult say, "That's not nice, Right?" No

Would an eight year old? Yes

Would an adult walk around everywhere with a pet chimp? No
Would a lonely eight year old? Possibly.

Would an adult have three hour phone call with a child about cartoons? No
Would an eight year old? Yes

Would an adult put a card on his nightstand that said to or from Doodoo head? No
Would an eight year old? Possibly

Would an adult tell people he always wants to play hide and seek? No
Would an eight year old? Yes

Would an adult have statues of Mickey Mouse and Pinocchio for his room? No
Would an eight year old? Yes

Would an adult build a place like Neverland to live in? No
Would an eight year old child? Yes, if he could

Would an adult refuse to say any curse words because it's "not nice"? No
Would an eight year old? Yes

Would an adult tell a woman who his having a baby to use the words "fudge" or "shoot" instead of curse words? Not if he wanted to live long.
Would an eight year old? Yes

Would an adult use the words "doodoo" for "feces" in a television interview? No
Would an eight year old? Yes

Would an adult say he looked "stinky"?   No
Would an eight year old? Yes

Would an adult dress up as The Elephant Man and think he was in disguise? No
Would an eight year old boy? Yes

Would an adult think he could cure Hitler by talking to him? No
Would an eight year old boy? Yes

Would an adult have relationships with the opposite sex and be happiest just holding hands? No
Would an eight year old boy? Possibly

Would an adult grab a newborn baby and run out of the hospital "placenta and all"? No
Would an excited and desperate eight year old boy? Possibly

See the pattern? I hope so.

Would an adult have a girlfriend/boyfriend relationship and be considered normal? Yes
Could an eight year old boy have a girlfriend/boyfriend relationship? YES!

It's called Puppy Love. Remember that? Did Michael have Puppy Love relationships? YES, he did. (Later in his life he also had real love feelings as an adult because his right side was nearly his actual age. I will explain that later)

Did he also like hanging around with young boys? YES, he did. That is because in most ways a great part of him was a normal eight year old boy and it would have been a "natural state of being" for him to hang out with those boys his own age. Michael hung out with children because he was one.

Now, here is the big Kahuna…

Here is the coup de grace.

NORMAL eight year old boys…

Do   Not   Have   Sex.

Chapter 6

The Adult and the Little Boy

When I first heard Michael's nurse saying those famous words I thought the story would be that he was simply a handicapped boy who was groomed and put on stage. What I found was such a different story. I found a person who was a stunning human being.

Michael was born a brilliant child beyond his ability to sing and dance. It was unusual for a child to be so brilliant but not unheard of by any means. He was not the only child born so far above the norm. Some celebrities, for example, were able to speak in numerous languages as children. Jodie Foster had a reported IQ of 132 and graduated magna cum laude from Yale. James Woods had a reported IQ of 180 and got a scholarship to MIT. Natalie Portman is fluent in five languages. Was this child that bright? I believe he was.

Being brain injured was also not unheard of. Children get injured all the time. My classrooms were filled with them. The students in my classroom were injured and normal but could have just as easily been injured and brilliant as Michael was.

Michael once said that he saw a handicapped person and wondered if that could be his situation. But most people with left brain impairments could not be spotted in the normal situation which is why Michael could never see one and say that was him. Except for their inability to make logical decisions they look like you and me.

Is it unusual for a child to be brilliant and brain injured? Yes, that would be unusual but still definitely possible.

The Brilliant Adult:

"I was raised on stage. I am happy on stage. I could sleep on stage..." When Michael was on stage he was using only his right brain and memory. Logical decisions were not needed and he was secure and happy. He was also for the most part his actual age. He was strong and powerful and in charge.

Walking around in daily life, hugging dying children, speaking poetry, telling stories and being loving uses the right brain and memory. Because of this a person in his daily life who is not sharing business dealings with Michael or engaged in similar things would most of the time not see the little boy.

As I make that statement I can picture his family saying that the above statement is not true. They would be saying that he was childlike at home with his parents and siblings and that would be true. Here are the reasons why he would be childlike in front of them. First, the brilliant side of him would not be able to convey itself to them because they simply would not have understood it. He was intellectually much higher then they were but he didn't know that he was above those around him. To him he was just different from them and would never be able to communicate. Second, and most importantly, he was the child in the beginning of his life to them and to change to the adult would have required a logical contemplation which he was not capable of. In other words, he was stuck in a childlike mode unable to logically break out.

I am going to use two poems written by Michael and one quote by him to show the brilliant adult he was. You will see a side of him never reported in the tabloids. You will see a person with an exceptional vocabulary and the ability to use it with the proficiency of an artist. You will see a brilliant Michael Jackson.

The Elusive Shadow

Even tho I traveled far
The door to my soul stayed ajar
In the agony of mortal fear
Your music I did not hear
Thru twisting roads in memory lane
I bore my cross in pain

It was a journey of madness
Of anguish born in sadness
I wandered high and low
Recoiled from every blow
Looking for that stolen nectar
In my heart that long-lost scepter
In all those haunted faces
I searched for my oasis

In a way it was in a drunken craze
A cruel hysteria, a blurry haze
Many a time I tried to break
This shadow following me I could not shake
Many a time in the noisy crowd
In the hustle and bustle of the din so loud
I peered behind to see its trace
I could not lose it in any place
It was only when I broke all ties
After the stillness of the shrieking cries

In the depths of those heaving sighs
The imagined sorrow of a thousand lies
I suddenly stared in your fiery eyes
All at once I found my goal
The elusive shadow was my soul

Breaking Free

All this hysteria, all this commotion
Time, space, energy are just a notion
What we have conceptualized we have created
All those loved, all those hated

Where is the beginning, where's the end
Time's arrow, so difficult to bend
Those broken promises, what they meant
Those love letters, never sent

Michael's quote:

"Our children are the most beautiful, most treasured of our creations.
And yet, every minute at least 28 children die. Today our children are
at risk or being killed by disaster and by the violence of war, guns,
abuse and neglect. Children have few rights and no-one to speak for
them. They have no voice in our world. God and nature has blessed me
with a voice. Now I want to use it to help children speak for
themselves. I have founded the Heal The World Foundation to be the
voice of the voiceless: The children."

The baby boy born a family in Gary, Indiana so long ago was not only right brain brilliant but left brain intelligent or left brained normal.

Then one day that left brain ability was...

GONE

The Little Boy:

"…When I'm off (stage) it is another story. It's hard to relate to people in everyday life." Michael Jackson"

Michael could not relate to people in everyday life because they expected him to be his chronological age but he was still a boy. He said it so many times but we didn't hear him. Michael enjoyed being the little boy as any little boy would and when he was with children he was not pressured to be what he could not be and do what he could not do.

The little boy was a ball and chain around the neck of the adult Michael except for the fact that he liked being that little boy.

When Robin Williams told a story of his drug addiction and he was asked if he wanted cocaine by someone he replied, "Yes". Robin stopped taking the drug years before but still wanted it because it was something that made him happy. As he once stated he would always want that drug but it was not the thing he should be doing. It was in fact a ball and chain that he liked that tempted him all of his life.

Michael was similarly held down by the child as Robin Williams was held down by that drug. Both offered happiness and kept popping up in life. For Michael the little boy brought happiness, and though he wanted to be an adult and be as others and was an adult in many ways, the little boy would always be there.

Unlike the Robin Williams story the weight on Michael that kept him down was "natural". It was a 'Natural State of Being" for Michael to be a little boy and for the boy to hold down the adult for as long as the little boy was still a little boy. In the normal educational peer pressured environment of school the little boy would have grown. Because

Michael had too few hours growing from his peers and understanding his situation, he stayed a little boy.

Since the normal brilliant adult was undamaged the adult would grow but the little boy would always be the "shadow he could not shake". Michael was an adult who wanted a normal relationship with a woman which was the reason he lamented about the "love letters, never sent". It was also the reason that he could not sing the song "She's out of my life" without crying no matter how many attempts to the point that they just left the crying in the song. At the same time the little boy wanted a relationship with his peers as a little boy normally would. To top it all off almost every child he befriended grew up and left him behind.

All of this left him alone.

So what really happened in that secret room mentioned in the first pages of this book? Surely, if little boys were allowed in there someone would have let the cat out of the bag in all those years. Who entered that room "packed with military-style costumes, children's toys and books"? What happened beyond the door down the narrow carpeted stairwell lined with rag dolls descending into a secret chamber? What happened in the twisted version of a young child's bedroom with the bed adorned with pillow cases imprinted with Peter Pan's face and the word "Neverland"? Who spoke on the Mickey Mouse telephone? Who put the pictures on the wall of smiling diapered (left brain undeveloped) babies?

Who lived in there? Who slept there? A lonely, lonely little boy.

Chapter 7

The Story
(as I believe it to be)

It is hard to comprehend that Michael could write such profound things and still be a child. In order to understand how this can happen you need to know the story.

On August 29, 1958 a beautiful child was born to a typical family in a typical small town in Gary, Indiana. But this child was not your typical child. This child was talented. This child was gifted. This child was loving. This child was brilliant, truly, truly brilliant. They named him Michael.

Unfortunately Michael did not fit in the family in which he was born and would spend his life with that brilliance being something that set him apart from them. He was never aware of what set him apart from his family. He just knew it was there.

Michael also had an extraordinary memory as was reported by many who knew him. Memory along with other things brings about a higher IQ. In addition, Michael knew from an early age that the things Joe Jackson did were wrong. He fought back and once as little boy threw his shoe at him. The others in the family just accepted Joe's vicious behavior. Not Michael. Michael was too smart and too loving for acceptance.

Michael watched his brothers being practiced as a band by his father every night when he was five years old. He knew he could do what his father was asking for from the band. He once voluntarily performed at his kindergarten Christmas pageant singing "Climb Every Mountain" from The Sound of Music with a talent that brought tears to the eyes of his teacher.

One fateful day he made the mistake of telling his father that he could do what the others were doing and that he should join the band. That ended up being a very bad thing for Michael.

The following was stated by Michael's kindergarten teacher, Felecia Childress. "My heart ached for him because I remember the joy that he had mixing with his little friends, but it was so short lived. He didn't have time to be a child. He just had to leave all of that behind and go to the serious part of life. And, that bothered me because I felt you know that's the way you learn so much about your relationships; is how you play."

The day that Joe Jackson realized that he had a star in Michael was the day he was forced to stop being a child. The joy his teacher spoke of was no longer. Michael once stated that he watched children play from the window of a car and wished he was there too.

With talented Michael at the lead, every night became a rehearsal with Joe Jackson standing over the boys with belts and iron cords to make sure they did what they were told. While other little boys were being punished with five minute timeouts and complaining at the lose of those few minutes of play, Michael was suffering a timeout that lasted for his entire childhood.

No more monkey bars. No more swings. No more playing tag with his school friends. No more joy in "mixing with his little friends". Michael would often talk about how he just wanted to play instead of doing what would be considered his job. When other children would be playing on the playground Michael would be "working". But that was not the worse part.

Michael's and his brothers slept in the same bedroom in a little house in Gary, Indiana. In the warm bed that he shared with his brother, Marlon he was warm and secure. Then, as he stated later, a loud bang would come through the door and startle them out of a sound sleep. It was the monster on the other side telling them to get out of their warm beds to do what? To go to work.

Gary Indiana was not Florida. The nights were very cold and probably the room itself was not warm. The little boy and his brothers had to get up in the middle of the night and get dressed to travel in a cold car to whatever the father had planned for the cold night.

They would either drive to whatever destiny was awaiting them or fly. Driving would mean that night that other children were sleeping in their warm beds Michael and his brothers were traveling in a cold uncomfortable car probably sleeping on the seat as they drove. My grandson is the same age as Michael was when this happened has a favorite stuffed tiger named Billy and a blanket with a torn corner that he loved to hold in the night. I wonder if Michael was able to bring his stuffed animal or blanket. I wonder if he even had one.

Half asleep, terrified Michael would have had to get on planes for some of the gigs. So on those days he was woken from a deep sleep, dragged into a car, woken when they got there to find that he had to go on a terrifying plane ride. Michael was terrified of planes all of his life and needed "assistance" in coping with his fear. So here this five year old terrified little boy who was sleeping only minutes before was forced to go on the horrifyingly loud plane in the middle of the cold dark night. The first Jackson movie showed a terrified Michael fighting not to get on the plane.

When they got to the place to perform Michael and the other boys had to be awake and in top shape for putting on a show. Being tired was not an option if they didn't want to be beaten later. I am sure the theater was not a warm cozy place for a child to get dressed and Michael would have rather been home in his warm bed.

Some time during his early life Michael suffered an injury that left him unable to use the part of the brain that deals with logic as his extraordinary memory and right brain remained intact. Since "playing" which his former teacher called " way to form and understand relationships" was removed from Michael for the next twenty years and his disability kept him from making sense of it all Michael didn't understand how to relate to peers and called his being finally allowed to have friends in his late twenties "new" to him.

This "serious part of life" namely work continued without play until he was into his twenties. The five minute timeouts that were unbearable for my five year old grandson lasted for over ten years for Michael. Michael spoke of being very lonely and walking the streets hoping to find someone to talk to. No one was there. But the person he need would have had to have been a very good special education teacher who was probably home working on lesson plans or a handicapped adult as he was who was probably home in a warm bed thinking about his next day of school or work.

This brilliant child who spent his later days reading in the back of the bus on his way to gigs when his brothers were horsing around in the middle of the bus was extraordinary from day one. He knew beyond the norm and would have been an extraordinary person.

In his twenties he finally had his first chance of having friends. By then he was an adult and having friends meant having friends who were younger than him and in fact still children. Those beings were like Michael because his brain injury, lack of education and appropriate peers kept him a child. But those children were few and far between and Michael, being a truly social person, had to fill his world with people.

58

His large bedroom was filled with games, arcades and facsimiles of people in the from of manikins.

At age twenty seven Michael was forced to leave the home he shared with his parents. The home was actually his home but he left them to live in it when he left. He didn't want to leave and stated that he was still "just a boy" but the move took place. I believe that this was done because it looked bad career wise for him to still be living with his parents at such an age. The action of trading Michael's welfare for his career began.

At the time of the move he was still working extreme hours and still lonely. With no parents there and no siblings Michael brought his manikins to his new home and filled the emptiness with a chimp that be brought with him everywhere..

Michael can be seen contemplating often in pictures and stated how lonely he was repeatedly to no avail. He searched and studied to try to find out what the emptiness was he was feeling but was never able to uncover the problem. Later in his life he was told that he should write his memoirs and his said he couldn't because he was still trying to figure it all out. For the next 40 years he was still trying to figure it all out, never to reach that goal.

What made this situation unusual was the fact that Michael was not educated to cope with the situation and was left floundering in a world he did not understand. In the normal world he would have been properly educated and would have done just fine.

I spoke before about the "natural state of being" meaning the natural progression of learning through play with peers ones own age. Michael was programmed as we all are to play as a child then grow little by little as we play to become an adult. That natural programming that was interrupted by work, celebrity and injury was still taking place as it should have in Michael. This forced him to want to play which would have simply made him a big kid except for the fact that those he related to had to be left brained equal which meant that play had to take place with children.

Michael's attraction to children I am sure alarmed those who took care of him. I believe many of the handlers of Michael thought those children to be in danger or possibly be in danger. This was a dilemma for the people in charge of him. I remember reading that Michael was often away and that when people including children would come to see him he was often working or away. He actually spent little time at Neverland considering that he lived there.

As I read I realized that there was a conflict going on. Michael needed to be with children and attempted to do so as much as possible. His handlers were charged with keeping him from children. To do so they had him running all over the world in tours or visiting dying children in hospitals all over the world. He willingly visited with those children from his heart which was typical Michael.

But he was human and the need to learn from play was tugging at him at all times. I am sure he wanted and stated that he needed to live a life he needed to live and I believe that he handlers told him that he had a responsibility and obligation to help and heal those children. That would be the only thing they could say to make him give up his life for them. They had to tug at his huge heart and his huge love for mankind. That is what they did and that was what gave Michael the idea that he could and had to heal the world.

Michael had some friends and some stayed friends with him his whole life but even if they did they grew and he did not. So though they may have physically have kept in touch they were not cognitively in touch. This left Michael making the statement later in life that he really only had five friends.

One person Michael met was the first accuser. That boy became Michael's friend before he was a world wide celebrity. That boy, like myself, had an unusual understanding of people like Michael and

Michael would follow him everywhere he went causing him to one time tell Michael he could not follow him because he was going to the bathroom. For Michael this boy was the first and only person to enter his life. This boy broke through the nearly twenty year loneliness making him the only person in the world to Michael and Michael asked him to stay at Neverland with him forever.

The statement by Michael of this boy staying with him forever did not mean that the boy would not grow up. What Michael meant was for the boy to always understand him and not be what Michael called "conditioned". Being conditioned was what the previous friends did and what grown ups did. Being conditioned meant seeing the things Michael did all wrong and not understanding him. If he had that one person he would no longer need the chimp and the manikins and the pictures of babies on his wall.

One time in an interview Debbie Rowe said that she picked Michael up on her motorcycle and they sneaked out. Then they "got caught". What did she mean by that? He was probably in his late twenties and early thirties. Did John Travolta have to sneak out when he as a celebrity in his late twenties and early thirties? What would have happened if he "got caught"? It was obvious by that statement that Michael was imprisoned.

As time went on Michael was growing. He considered himself a father figure. At this same time the tabloids crucified him. Everything he did was reported to them and nothing was positive. He wondered who told every move he made. He trusted almost no one and rightfully so. A reporter for the tabloids was on the television and stated that people thought that it was the reporters that gave most of the stories to the tabloids but it was, in reality, friends and family. So, so many who hung around with Michael were not friends.

Neither were we. Michael was getting older and wrinkles were beginning to set in. Michael, having no clue what the heck we wanted from him knew one thing. He knew that one wrinkle spotted on his face would be world wide tabloid news. So sad but so true.

So surgery after surgery was performed in Michael's usual modus operandi to please us without him actually knowing what it was that would please us. I guess the truth is that nothing would have pleased us.

Michael tried to grow though being with children, handlers tried to keep him from children for their safety and theirs, women tried to mother him, people tried to steal from him, friends walked away from him eventually, gatekeeper wanted him to seem crazy so the public would never know he was handicapped. All of this happened while Michael held dying children, tried to save all those he could, tried to teach children around him all he could and tried to write to us or tell us what he was feeling.

No wonder he said he was having a "terrible life".

Chapter 8

Other Peter Pans

I worked with these students for almost fifty years now. My specialty was bizarre behaviors. I was often given the most bizarre cases which made understanding Michael so simple since his disability was so small. Those behaviors, no matter how strange they seemed, always became behaviors that were not really bizarre after all. All of them made perfect sense.

I would like to give you an example of such a situation but please, please understand that this person was both brain impaired and way more impaired than Michael. Still it is a good example of bizarre not being bizarre after all so I am going to tell it to you.

I worked with a student who, remember, had much more severe disabilities than Michael affecting both sides of the brain. His paperwork labeled him, along with other things, paranoid schizophrenic. I worked with him for 8 years. He would tell us he would burn his mother and that was what he had to do. Remember again he was very, very disabled. He was not at all in the category of Michael but I want to show you how what seemed bizarre can make perfect sense.

Members in his family were fanatic horror movie watchers. His mother, as it turned out, really was a pretty evil person. She was so evil that he didn't want us to meet her for fear we would be influenced by her and his security would be lost. When we did finally meet her he paced back and forth in a sweat. When she left he looked at us in fear. His demeanor changed when he realized that we were the same after we met her as we were before. That was quite revealing for us.

In horror movies, the way to get rid of the evil person was to burn them. Therefore, he was telling what had to be done. Because he told people his mother should be burned he was labeled "Paranoid Schizophrenic". No one told him that those movies were not real. On the day he told me to do something he had seen in the horror movie because he was mad at me, he was shocked when I did it and did not disappear or blow up or whatever. It shocked him that I had the nerve to do it and I thought he was going to faint from fear. That was the lesson that cured him and made us realize what the problem really was for him. When he was to leave our program he said to me, "I'm going to give you a great big hug." I said, "And I will be waiting for it." I never saw him again but I know he was okay, he had no more inkling to burn anyone and I knew that he made perfect sense not only to me but to himself.

Even for this very disabled young man what seemed so bizarre was as logical as possible when you understood.

Whether you believe that Michael was horrible, terrible, bad with money, a great businessman, weird or wonderful, you have to admit that there were often times that his logic did not fit the norm for an adult man. His lack of logic made him fodder for the tabloids and caused him to get in a lot of trouble.

Some students were injured and you would never know it by looking at them like the boy who had no obvious injuries on the outside but was a student of mine because he got hit in the head by a truck. I am sure it could not have been going very fast but it doesn't take much to cause a lot of damage. That young man had left side impairment as well.

I want to give you an idea of the personality of that young man in the above paragraph so you can get an idea of how normal he was in addition to being disabled.

Each of my students had a computer to use personally in our setting. We didn't watch them like hawks but we did tell them that if something inappropriate came on the computer via the Internet they were to let us know. We went out of the room for a trip and when we came back he went back to his computer. My assistant went with him. When my assistant touched the mouse the screen came up and up came some heavy duty porn. I was pretty angry with my student and told him so saying that I trusted him and that he knew to report anything like that to us. He said, "I know and I tried but, but my, my eyes, they, they wouldn't move." How can you argue with that? It goes to show some normalcy and, well normalcy is really the word showing through in this left brain impaired young man.

Megan's story shows how people with left brain injuries think and can communicate but can't exactly know what is right to do. Megan was very shy when I first met her but with the right teaching grew to be a strong adult. Megan was a lot like Michael. So, Michael would have grown too had he been given the chance.

In order to understand these people you have to know Megan. It should be a requirement in life that everyone meet Megan, a beautiful girl with the face of an angel. Megan, not her real name, was also a student of mine.

I was at a meeting once with Megan and other professionals. The psychologist was present and told the teacher that Megan should be taught things like not to take other people's medicine. Megan, outgoing and beautiful just like Michael, was very quiet as I walked her back to her classroom. I asked her what was wrong and she said, quite loudly I might add, "What does she think I am, stupid? She thinks I need to be taught not to take other people's medicine. What does she think I am a child?" Those were her exact words. I couldn't argue. About a month later she came up to me at lunch and said, "I saw that lady here and she I think owes me an apology." I proudly said, "Go for it". Once she knew it was the right thing to do, she did. She walked right up to that big lady in the big suit and said, "You owe me an apology." "I do? Why?" the lady replied, I'm sure quite shocked. "Because you made me feel stupid in my meeting telling my teacher that I have to be taught not to take other people's medicine. I'm not a child."

Megan was amazing. Here is another story about her.

When she would have a problem she would always come to tell me. I would tell her that she needed to tell her dad who was her only caretaker. Her response, "Daddy doesn't care". This ended up being somewhat true as it often was about these types of people, that they tried to tell what many didn't hear. Daddy didn't care about the person that was Megan. Daddy fed her and Daddy bought her clothes but Daddy didn't see the being that was there. He didn't see the teenager either. At age 17 she got a toothache. I told her to tell her father. She said that she did but "Daddy didn't care". We were forced to get a person higher up than us to "encourage" Dad to take her to the dentist.

One day she was supposed to go to a job interview. It was a job she really wanted. He promised to take her but at the last minute said he wouldn't. At that point she knew that her father could not be trusted to help her with her life.

When she told me what happened I told her that one day the time would come when she would not have my assistance any longer. I told her that when she is 18 she belongs to herself not Daddy. This beautiful teenager stood up to her father and made all the plans to leave him including having all the finances transferred to an agency that would care for her. She, like Michael, was not good with money. When it came to only a few days from her leaving he begged her to stay. He promised that he would do the things she needed. She said, "You lied to me once. Why should I believe you won't lie to me again?" See the "story"? Yes, this special needs girl who has had boyfriends since then but does not like to be kissed said such a profound thing.

This last story of Megan shows her growth and struggle with the right brain "story" that did not make left brain sense due to her limits. Here is what happened. Megan is a tiny black girl. Many times we struggled to help her with her hair in the room. It was the normal hair of a black person. One day she brought in a book and plopped it on my desk. And I mean she really plopped it on my desk. The book title was, "I Love My Hair" and on the front was the picture of a black girl with a smiling face. She stared at me and I knew it needed my attention so I stopped what I was doing to read her book. When I was done I called her over and said, "I don't like your book." She smiled a huge smile. "Do you like your hair?" "No, I hate my hair. That girl says she can do anything with her hair but she has the same hair as me. I can't do anything with it."

That was the end of the conversation but for Megan it was a turning point. Her right brain story telling mind could not understand the story because it made no sense. When I was able to relay to her that the girl out rightly lied the fact that she lied became part of the story and made sense so she was happy. You and I would simply say as I did, "what a bunch of bull." But Megan was not able to do that until I gave her the ability to do so. This story preceded the above story where Megan told the psychologist off and stood up to her father. This story made her realize that authority people, who are what people who write books would be, could lie or be wrong. If only Michael knew what was happening, his right brain could have made sense of it all.

Welcome to my world of right brain works but left brain has difficulty. Welcome to the world of someone who could tell the story and tell the feeling but not logically know if it was the right thing to do. Welcome to my world and welcome to the world, I believe, of Michael Jackson.

Chapter 9

The Great Illusion

The Great Illusion for all of us was that Michael was a great businessman, inventor, writer, etc. The Greater Illusion was that he was in all ways an adult, childlike but still an adult.

Michael was a brilliant right brain adult who was driven to succeed. He truly was driven not only to earn money and be number one as it was drilled into him to be but he was driven to find the answers to who he was and what was wrong. This right brain Michael was entirely an adult and it was often the Michael we saw.

I have read enough books now about Michael to hear the criticism of this concept before it is even spoken. Those who knew him would say I am crazy. They would say he was a businessman. Those who knew and were opposed to him would say he was a vicious businessman who cared only about himself. He was cunning and mean.

When Michael was in school he told his teacher that he didn't need to learn math because he would have managers to do that for him. She must have thought that so cute for a five or six year old. Where would Michael have gotten that idea from? I can hear it. Michael is not doing well at math so Joseph tells Michael, "Don't worry about it.

You will have managers to do the math for you." There it is, the story that became Michael's to use throughout his life not only to avoid math but to start businesses by giving others the paperwork and business responsibilities. Michael says he wants to start a business and they say okay and do the work. That makes it seem like he started the business when he only had the right brain idea. Not an uncommon procedure actually.

Here is a quote from Mark Twain. "Give the man a reputation as an early riser and that man can sleep 'til noon."

Everyone and I mean everyone, thought Michael to be an adult, a childlike adult. Everyone started out from the premise that he was an adult and associated whatever business they had with him from that standpoint.

Interviewers would see him for only 20 minutes and hear what he may or may not have rehearsed to say. They were all trying to understand the adult sitting before them. After all he looked like an adult...sort of. He was a multimillionaire running multiple businesses. His ideas sold all over the world.

Wouldn't you have to be an adult to do all of those things? No, you would have to have extreme talent, luck, Professionals, Handlers and Gatekeepers. That's all you would need.

Take Diane Sawyer. She so tried to warn him of the danger of having little boys in his bedroom. She was speaking from a logic standpoint to an adult. He was listening and speaking from a story standpoint as an adult but when it came to the logic part he was a child. No way would their minds have met.

The illusion that Michael was a normal adult capable of normal decision making was believed by everyone including Michael. I read where he started a company called MJJ Productions. He made someone he knew vice president. But how much did Michael really do? Did he just give orders on what to buy and what he wanted? If so that would be right brain. In the music and video business he could succeed easily. The paperwork, the math, the money would be left brain and typically done by others. Therefore, being a businessman would fit the picture and promote the illusion.

Here is what I pictured happened and happened over and over in his "business" dealings. Michael gets this brainstorm, right brain creative brainstorm. For instance, he hears Paul McCartney tell the story of making money with other people's songs by purchasing them. Michael had already learned that he should own his own songs. So he decides to buy other people's songs. Paul made money this way. Why shouldn't he? Paul told the story and Michael made the story about him. Then he went to his business acquaintances and said start this company and do this or take the company that is already there and do this. Money is not object because he has no real concept of money. "Do it whatever it takes." he had been known to say. This is how he acquired the songs that are worth a fortune today.

Sometimes he got lucky and sometimes he didn't. It was that simple. "Michael is a ticking financial time bomb waiting to explode at any moment." [22]

I remember reading that at a meeting Michael started laughing and continued throughout the meeting. That makes sense to me. Meetings would have to be horribly boring for him and being so active he would have to do something. But when he was laughing though the meeting, what did they do? Well, the business managers must have been there and they knew what was going on so they would do it without him. He had the final say but that would be only, "Do you want to do this, Mike?"

One example is in the book, *Michael Jackson Behind the Mask*. The author stated, "Michael Jackson attempted to start a Holy War between the Jews and the Arabs...and it didn't work. The concept that this person who asked his friend who was thirteen, "What is your favorite curse word?" could plan to start a war between nations is ridiculous to me.

This eight year old boy had millions to deal with and spend. I don't know how many of us normal adults would know how to survive owning millions of dollars.

Don't forget for one second that Michael was very driven and had no idea that he was not capable of running a business like any other person. He DIDN'T KNOW he was not normal. He just knew he did weird things that made no sense to people. In his mind, he was the genius everyone around him told him he was. That is very, very important to understand. Michael was not trying to fool anyone. He honestly, honestly DIDN'T KNOW. He believed the illusion just like the rest of us.

If you think him a great businessman and a vicious person who didn't care about what people thought. If you thought him a user who just cared about himself, you still can't explain the chimp and the manikins.

Chapter 10

Acceptance and Perception

Family:

In one of my classes in psychiatry years ago the professor played a tape of an institutionalized patient who kept repeating the name Cynthia and the name John and the word "lemon". At that time Cynthia Lennon and John Lennon had just split up. It struck me funny that, though the patient's words were confused into other words and hidden, most of the class saw that the conflict had to do with relationship stability. The professor was so fixated on the big words and the analysis of the situation that he lost sight of the common answer. We, the whole class, knew it was "displacement" and we knew why. He, on the other hand, hadn't a clue. The point is that sometimes you can get so deep into something that you don't see the forest for the trees.

Here is the situation that the family was in if they understood what was going on with Michael. There is a good chance they didn't have the correct picture. If they did, that would be very, very sad.

Imagine that you were in the family, a brother of Michael's or his parent. As a young child there is little or no difference between someone who is normal and someone left brain impaired especially if they are so right brain capable. He, at five when he is still comparable in ability with other five year olds, is becoming a star. He can sing like a canary and dance with such talent. You see your child the star and your child the little boy before your very eyes.

As time goes on the gap gets bigger. Suddenly that little boy who is known for his talent and is meeting celebrities all over the world singing with the likes of Diana Ross is not behaving as the other brothers had at that age. You may have your doubts about him but maybe it would not be that obvious. Maybe what is happening is because he works into the night and can't do well in school because of it. He also spends a lot of time working. So he acts a bit immature. No big deal yet.

You have to add into the equation that that many years ago there was little understanding of these types of people and no understanding of left brain/right brain differences. This field is relatively new being maybe thirty years old.

Your child now an adult, likes to fill his room with manikins, arcades, toys. Things are beginning to seem weird.

I read once how Michael was on stage and his mother was in the audience when he came down from the stage and tried to get her to come on stage with him. He said she was so shy and she was crying and she said, "Look at you,.. so many people".

Suddenly he is a young adult and a renowned star. The world wants your little boy. Everything he does is successful and perceived as genius…except he walks around with a chimp.

By now you realize, if you haven't already that something is terribly wrong. What do you do? You don't really know exactly what is wrong. You know he is like a child. You know he is very talented and writes songs. You don't know what to do with him. He is certainly different than anyone you had seen before when you look at the things he does. Even if you ask him why he is doing what he is doing, he doesn't answer you. You don't know how to handle the things he does and you don't know what he will do next. Your best bet is to keep him close but he is older and people are beginning to wonder why he is still at his parents' house.

Being so talented he knows too that he can do his own music better than anyone especially his father. He is also being sought after by others who want to control him and run his career and he has already seen that they can do a great job as Berry Gordy had done.

He moves out and is now an older adult and he likes hanging around with children. He will do things like hold hands with them no matter what their age. He will invite people like Emmanuel Lewis to the Grammy awards along with Brooke Shields and then give Emmanuel a kiss on the cheek as he goes into the Grammy awards. The bizarre behavior goes on and on and you don't know what it will bring next. Is he a good boy? Yes. Would he hurt someone? No. Would he be able to realize that there are bad people in the world who could look in his face and do horrible things to him? No, not yet. Would he do things that could be misconstrued due to impaired judgment? Absolutely. Can you stop it now that he is an adult, on his own and in the hands of strangers and has more money than you ever thought possible? No.

Members of the family saw "Uncle Michael" as a joker. As one of Tito's children said, "One minute he would be Uncle Michael playing practical jokes and the other he was Superman." One brother said, "We just thought our brother was gay." But that concept didn't work either.

Jermaine once wrote that Michael was "a child". I believe that the Jackson family believed, as Jermaine did, that it was simply that Michael was a child who never grew up. I don't think it occurred to them that there was actually a physical situation that made him as he was and even in the situation with Jermaine calling him a child, he was trying to reason with him. If he knew what was wrong with Michael he would have known that it would not be possible to reason with him. Michael could not reason. Reasoning takes left brain action.

So, what do you do? You're a bit used to his antics by now but the world is not and they are brutal. Do you tell them or him there is something wrong? You are not sure what is going on either. Maybe you realize he is disabled and maybe you don't. What do you do? Truthfully, if I were in that position and didn't have the knowledge I have about this situation, I have no idea what I would do.

So many families and parents have said, "I don't understand this" and "I don't understand that". Michael must have been so confusing to his family. I would think they loved him. But I am sure they did not understand things like why he needed to bring a chimpanzee everywhere he went.

Joe Jackson once stated that he didn't understand why Michael was always so lonely when he had tons of nephews and cousins.

I need to say that family confusion was a very large part of my work. Often, so very often, family members would guess at why this was done or that was done and have a completely wrong concept. Michael was a kind person so he didn't do this but I have seen some students use their disabilities to make a parent jump through hoops and laugh about it. They were impaired, not stupid and they didn't always have a heart. Michael had a great heart. I am happy to say that.

The gap between the abilities of a five year old and a five year old with left brain disabilities is very small at first. As the child grows the gap gets larger. It is unknown to me when the Jackson family actually realized there was something seriously wrong with Michael. I would like to assume it was after he had made a fortune being Michael Jackson and I would think that it posed quite the dilemma.

Though it is hinted to in the Jackson movie where Joe Jackson tells Michael he needs to stick to music because of a bad deal he made with selling candy, it does not show as a very serious situation.

I would assume Michael's family didn't realize the price his disability would cost later. I would also assume and hope that they didn't realize that the cause of his extreme loneliness would be his not being with those who were like him or understanding there were others that were like him. Maybe the family didn't realize there were others like Michael. I hope that is the case.

Friends:

Adult friends accepted Michael as he was. They saw the good side of him and just thought "that's Michael", he's a practical joker, that's just him. To understand what it was about him would not have been their thing. Most who would analyze Michael said he was "eccentric". That was the term used over and over in the things I read. Michael was just Michael. Michael was eccentric. For many of his friends he was a confusion they just accepted.

There were some people who knew him personally and just accepted that he did strange things but liked him anyway. After all he was probably the most liked guy ever by people who really knew him as a person not an icon or a business partner. With every thing I read or heard from those who really knew him he was very loved and liked. How many people can you say that about? And of course they would not want to do or say anything to damage his career or image.

The concept that he was a major businessman with tons of money played a major role in them just accepting his unusual ways. How could they be thinking that there was possibly something seriously wrong with him? Remember the image of the icon is very, very in your face, so how could he be anything but an eccentric adult?

A huge problem for parents of my students is that when the student looks like there is nothing wrong they have a more difficult time in life with what people demand from them. For Michael, the groomers, choreographers, handlers and his extreme and beautiful talents added to the belief that all was well, until it kept falling apart.

Then there were the outsiders who were simply totally confused by the guy who was so together and falling apart at the same time. They spent their time trying to fit a round peg in a square hole and got only tons of speculation as to what was going on. If you come from the wrong premise to start with imagine how many ways you can go wrong. Think of the equation of two plus two which we all know has the answer of four and now think of the number of wrong answers you can come to with that same equation if you discount four as the answer. That would make infinite as the number of answers to why Michael did the things he did and they are out there.

Perception is everything until truth oozes out.

Neverland workers:

Those who worked with Michael saw him for himself if they worked at Neverland. But Michael was the boss. He was not just the one who paid their salaries. It was not money that made them accept the illusion of what he was. It was the fact that they were workers, average people and Michael was a millionaire or multimillionaire. Michael was a giver of millions of dollars to charity. Michael was a person who invited Gregory Peck to his house and shook hands with Queen Elizabeth II. He had to be exceptional. That is the precept from which they began their relationship with Michael.

I once worked for a billionaire. I watched people try to make sense of the things he did from a standpoint of brilliance. I was one of them. I watched them try to make sense of something to only find that their logic did not work after all. What actions they saw different than actions we would have taken were seen as brilliant. He was in fact, human and the funny thing is, as I would come to learn, those brilliant actions were in reality just mistakes.

Professionals:

Coworkers in the entertainment field saw the right brain Michael come up with some great songs and great dance moves and such.

That Michael had talent was not in doubt. What we don't often realize is that life itself gives us the opportunity to make something small into something large if the opportunity presents itself. Michael wrote "don't stop 'til you get enough" with Randy's help. "I was walking around the house and I just started singing, "da-da-da-da-da-da da" and said, "Ah, that sounds kinda good". I kept singing it and gradually it came about. I went into the studio; we have a studio at home, a 24 track studio. Randy and I, I told Randy what to put down, what to play on the piano, and we did some percussion and some clapping and it turned out real funky. I played it for Quincy Jones and he loved it."

"I have nothing but love and admiration for Michael. Despite his gifts Michael Jackson was a tragic figure. I have nothing but love and admiration for Mike as a person and truly international and great star. But he often was sad and he was eccentric. Very sweet guy. Everyone who worked with Mike liked him." --John Landis, director of Thriller [23]

Entertainment professionals worked with Michael both extensively and intermittently. Those who worked with him a lot got to see him as he was and look beyond the facade of the Michael Jackson icon to see some of the real person. They, however, had no idea they were dealing with a handicapped child. To them he was just "childlike" or "eccentric" just as John Landis thought. Plus they just liked him as he was and didn't try to figure him out. Others saw the entertainer and accepted that he was just shy and eccentric and the famous icon... The Michael Jackson fans screamed for.

Professional interviewers:

Remember the quote from Mark Twain. Surely, it applies here. All of the professionals who interviewed Michael, book and magazine writers who wrote about him, tabloid people who wrote such crap about him assumed they were talking to a professional entertainer who was eccentric but still a successful adult.

The professionals who interviewed Michael tried repeatedly to understand him. They tried to understand and tried to warn him and tried to communicate but to no avail. But Michael, the left brain injured eight year old, was unable to understand.

Remember these interviewers are people who sit across from those who are the biggest names in politics, big deal entertainers, royalty and some tough people. They start off from the standpoint they always started from. Why wouldn't they?

It struck me funny that many started off trying to understand him and then often ended up being nurturing. I was certainly moved by Diane Sawyer's attempt to change his mind about having children sleep in his bed to keep him from getting into trouble again. She really tried and had a motherly care for him but, of course, it was not possible to reach him.

You have to remember that interviews are stories. Michael was great at storytelling. Not that they were lies. They were when he was trying to protect his life or career or when he was told not to tell something, but other than that they were the truth the best he could tell it.

I am going to quote excerpts from the book by Rabbi Shmuley Boteach and I know he may feel bad but he could not have helped Michael. Many people tried to help him. They were unable, and they were unable because of one thing. They did not have the knowledge to do so. They were not able to see past the adult picture to the child because they were not trained to do so and they did not know that he could be capable and disabled at the same time. As I would have been unable to help Michael medically because I wouldn't have had the knowledge, neither could they because they didn't have the understanding that it was possible to be the way he was.

Rabbi Shmuley Boteach in his book "The Michael Jackson Tapes" said that he went to the Toy Story movie with Michael and the kids. "I sat one row in front of Michael as he laughed uncontrollably throughout the movie. At first it struck me as juvenile. After all, this was a kid's film and I was attending only for the sake of my children. But to be honest, hearing Michael in fits of laughter in the seat behind me was liberating, like it was okay for adults to let their guard down and see the world through the innocent eyes of a child."

You see here an example, not that I want to put the good rabbi down but this example is too good to pass up, where the obvious is discarded for the illusion. At first he thought it juvenile because it was juvenile. Then he dismissed his first instinct for a rational opinion based on the fact that Michael was an adult, a businessman and an artist, mostly that he was an adult.

This is another example of a time when the Rabbi missed the clue. I don't mean to pick on him because he was a man who loved Michael. He really did but with the precept already there, there was no way to communicate what was really happening. I am using his actions as an example, because his book was the last one I read concerning Michael.

In reality there were so many examples from hundreds of professionals who missed the clues. Diane Sawyer missed the clue when Michael put Indian fingers behind Lisa's head for a joke. What adult would do that? The illusion was set in place by professional illusion makers, by our assumptions and also in large part because of the fact that Michael was so talented.

"The video for Michael's song "The Way You Make Me Feel" premiered on MTV on October 31. 1987. In it, Michael chases after a girl who continually runs away from him. He finally gets the girl at the end and they hug, to the great disappointment of the fans who wanted them to kiss. The hug was enough for Michael, however, who wanted to leave the rest to the viewer's imagination."

In this example, the explanation of why Michael avoided the kiss was justified. He, as a professional, wanted to leave it to the imagination. That would be the rationalization of an adult speaking of another adult who was a professional entertainer. In reality it was that eight year old boys really don't want to kiss girls. This rationalization and attempt at understanding was done all the time.

Fans:

Perception is everything. Well, perception is almost everything. None if this would have happened if Michael didn't have the extraordinary talent that people don't deny he had. Still perception is everything until truth oozes out. For the fans all most cared about was the Michael Jackson that was a Godlike image. The image, the icon was a small piece of what Michael was but that is what they wanted to see and what they wanted to believe to be real.

For Michael it was a hard place to be in. On one hand he loved having the fans there admiring his work. On the other hand they were his prison guards.

"I love the fans," he would sometime say.

"You feel like you're spaghetti among thousands of hands. They're just ripping and pulling your hair. And you feel that any moment you're gonna break"

You will see in later chapters that that is exactly how they were. And they called him "Wacko". I had to laugh at that. I'll bet he never clawed at his face and screamed all night so a person could not sleep. I'll bet he never ripped at a person or pulled their hair.

The truth is that he loved the fans but they loved the icon. As Michael said, "That's not me." Charlie Chaplin actually once said basically the same thing to his brother.

In reality, the fans just wanted the illusion. I hope they have learned that the show is just a show and the person does not belong to them.

Perception:

"Michael was a smart boy" said the teacher who only had him for 3 months.

Now how could she have known that? After all he was woken up in the middle of the night on most school days to perform until three or four in the morning and then came to school with a few hours sleep if he was lucky. Boy, it would take a hell of a person to be smart in school at six years old under those circumstances. But there was the statement.

I want to add two things to this that drove me crazy.

One was the glove. According to Cecily Tyson, Michael had the glove made to cover the irregular color on his hands due to Vitiligo. He also always bandaged fingers on his right hand. Maybe it was also to cover the bandages he needed due to Raynaud's disease. But whichever it was he wore it for medical purposes. It then became a trademark. How silly. If it were a crutch he needed or a cast on his arm would they have sold his crutch or cast for fifty thousand dollars on Ebay? Would they have buried him with a crutch if he was unable to walk and used a crutch? Did they bury him with his umbrella?

Why then the glove? Unlike the white socks it was not him. Still we need our golden idols. So sad.

Second was the Penguin. After Michael died the public saw him during rehearsals moving in a strange way shaking his arm back and forth. They immediately named the move "The Penguin" and people started doing it everywhere. But the move was not graceful and Michael was always graceful in his dancing. It was very ungraceful actually. I believe that it was his way of bringing blood to his hands or fingers and they just video taped it and ran with it. Everyone followed. If I am right it shows the power of the illusion and the people who just want to believe and follow.

I want to end this chapter with this quote from John Landis. Although it shows his wrong concept of Michael it also shows his love for him. I had seen in videos John Landis playing with Michael and caring for him and I have to say that I am happy Michael knew him and that John got to tickle Michael on the bottom of his feet!

John Landis: "...I got a call from Michael. He had just seen An "American Werewolf in London'. And he basically called me and said he wanted to turn into a monster. So that eventually became Thriller. "I have nothing but love and admiration for Michael in terms of as a person and truly an international and great star I was aware of that from the beginning but he often was sad and he was eccentric, you know, Once we were at Universal at my office and I said let's go up to the back of the future ride its very cool. And he said, "Okay but I have to put on a disguise." And I said, "Mike, no one will bother you." And he said, "No, I have to put on a disguise." So he went to the car and he came back with a red satin surgical mask, this big impresario hat and a cape. And I just said, "OK Mike, no one will notice you now." He was really outrageous and a very sweet guy. Every one who worked with Michael was very fond of him. He was a lovely person. I find it sad". [23]

Chapter 11

Money, Handlers, Gatekeepers

I remember the first time I saw Michael pose for pictures and it reminded me of when he told his horse to "give them a profile shot". It made me realize how much of a show everything was.   As a regular person it's so hard to imagine being on stage virtually every moment of every day of your life.

I don't know what to tell you about these people. People like this never touched my life.   I know Elizabeth Taylor said that she felt owned by the studio. I read that somewhere.   I know they existed and I know that they helped hide the secret about Michael, some on purpose and most not.

I am writing of them because they were part of keeping the secret and promoting the illusion.   I am writing this book to clear the name of a little boy who was charged with things of which only an adult should have been charged.

There was a ton of money involved in Michael Jackson as we all know. Millions and millions of dollars attracts millions and millions of rotten people.   It also attracts lots of good people. It also attracts people who were there to protect and grow the product, namely Michael Jackson.

Things would have been so much easier if the good guys would wear white hats and the bad guys would wear black hats and when the good guys turned to bad guys their hats would turn gray. That surely would have made Michael's life easier. He had no idea who was a friend and who was not for the most part. In all my studies, most times neither did I.

I would have loved to be able to write this chapter saying that I knew who they all were. There were too, too many and there was too much confusion Michael caused himself without knowing why or how.

The story starts out with the product called Michael Jackson. The public loved the product. I know because I was someone who loved the little boy who burst on the stage years ago. So what was the product really? There was the fabulous singer and dancer. There was the cute young man. And there was the powerful adult who could command the stage. Those things made Michael Jackson the million dollar product. I know because I was a customer.

Of Michael Jackson the dancer and entertainer there was no doubt of his salability. No person I have ever met or heard from or read about denied his fabulous talent. So that is a given.

Michael Jackson the cute young man existed for a while thanks to the Handlers who dressed him and packaged him and marketed him. It was loss of skin color which was said to have been the result of Vitiligo that caused him to be so questioned about his looks. Had he not had such white skin his surgeries would have not been so obvious and he might have been able to slide by.

Michael Jackson the powerful adult entertainer who commanded the stage was what really brought in the money. It was also the part of Michael Jackson, "the product", that was in jeopardy when he did things like invite boys in his bed, hang around with a chimp, be a "virgin".

John Branca seemed to me in what I read to be the lead businessman behind the workings of the businesses of Michael Jackson. Michael had the ideas but John executed them. "Michael studied every angle before reaching a decision-or at least he had someone else do it for him, namely John Branca."

"Indeed, Michael had the wisdom to surround himself with brilliant people, and allow them to do their jobs without interference."

Michael's stage presence showed a man who was powerful and in control. He looked the part and acted the part. His everyday persona did not fit and did not support the illusion of the powerful man seen on stage. "...Michael's music has had a sensual edge over the years, and his dancing has often been suggestive, he was not sexually adventurous as a young man". [24]

At first I wanted to name this chapter "How they did it." I wanted it to be a chapter about how you could take someone and groom them and dress them and put them in the right setting with great choreography and great music and use public relations persons and managers and handlers and on and on to make them a star.

As I went on I realized that a part of the situation that was important was also why they did it. There were so many people in the story that it was impossible to keep track of who really cared for Michael and who just wanted to keep the company called Michael Jackson, going.

And there was so...much...money.

The Workers:

The workers came and went. They did their jobs the best they could and thought all they were doing was right and what was right for

Michael. They would work with Michael doing videos and making music and unknowingly peppering his work with the logic that would keep the public in the dark about his abilities. They had no idea they were any part of keeping the truth from coming out. Some stole from him and some were honest. Some stayed and some left or were fired. They didn't know what was wrong with Michael. They assumed what most assumed: that he was eccentric and that eccentricity and his talent is what got him to stardom and to be a millionaire. What did Lisa Marie say? "He's an artist." They are not the topic of this chapter really.

I believe there were three types of players who kept the secret.

The first type in this instance were people who knew basically that there was something wrong with Michael and that he was really a child in an adult body, not just childlike. They just thought that was the way he was. There were the people who knew and loved him anyway who wanted his company or him to succeed for the sake of everyone including Michael. They were just people doing their job the best they could. People like the children's nanny Grace would probably be among them.

The Handlers:

The second type of players in the picture we will call the Handlers. That is actually the name for them. It was their job to keep the fires out and make sure Michael Jackson, the company, dressed like an icon, looked like an icon and behaved like an icon, went where he was assigned as the icon, kept in the public eye as an icon. This was a very hard job with the eight year old Michael who wanted to be free and who strived to be just a kid as he stated he was numerous times. They knew he was odd and that he did strange things. They knew they had to continually put out fires. To them, their adult boss was maybe spoiled, weird, eccentric, liked to hang with children and may be a child molester. I want to and really do think that they just thought he was an immature adult, uh and maybe a child molester. I want to think, and really do believe, that none of these people knew that he had a developmental impairment and that he would have been so happy and free if he knew.

It would have been the job of the Handlers to keep Michael from doing child things like using the word "doodoo". If you look at the 60 Minutes interview after his arrest you will see him saying "doodoo" then saying "feces" quickly after it. It would have been the job of the Handlers to make sure Michael knew to use the adult word. It would have been the job of the Handlers to keep him looking like an adult.

It would have been the job of the Handlers to make the public think that Michael was a good businessman. It would have been the job of the Handlers to make sure the public knew he had many companies and ran them himself. It would have been the job of the Handlers to make sure he looked good. The child along with his disease continually got in the way of that one.

Joe Jackson said, "Michael never cared about money." Why then did tabloids blame him for what was not paid? Whose job was it to handle the money then? Surely, not Michael's. But it was reported over and over that he did not do this money wise and he did not do that money wise. I am sure he said I want to use my money to go here and do this and that but to be intricately involved. No.

Those who knew Michael acted more like a child than the public realized had a job on their hands. It was the job of the Handlers to handle everything from money to his clothes to the press. It was their job to keep Michael from sabotaging himself. Perception is everything especially when you're the King of Pop. Not an easy job with someone like Michael who wanted to be close to people by nature and really was a child. Remember there is a lot of money at stake... millions and millions.

Like I said before, when I first realized what the story was with Michael I thought everyone knew the truth and were covering things up for money and cared nothing about Michael. I thought they hid his disabilities and let him flounder in the world alone.

In my research I found that, for the most part, that was not the case. Almost everyone I read about and everyone I heard speaking to him either tried to figure him out or believed he was just an eccentric adult that acted like a spoiled child. No one thought he was disabled, none of the Handlers, anyway. I was surprised about that, really.

The dilemma for the Handlers was that they were very close to Michael. They also didn't know that a person could be "capable' and "disabled" at the same time. They were normal people who went home to normal homes. They were professionals and businessmen.

With the number of boys that Michael had in his room and his bizarre behavior with them, I am sure they had their doubts about his innocence and his motives. On top of that his behavior in other matters must have made them wonder about his sanity. Like the man said," he was the weirdest man on the planet."

Gatekeepers:

It was the job of the Gatekeepers to keep the secret of the child that he really was from getting out. They could handle the odd stuff that came out but if the real truth came out that Michael was a disabled child it could have collapsed the empire. For them it would have been better if the world thought he was weird and crazy than handicapped.

They didn't care about Michael, disabled or not. Contracts for his music could have been worthless or worth less. There were the powers that would not let that happen. They were the Gatekeepers.

This was a news article about Tommy Mattola who was not considered by me to be a Gatekeeper.

"Mottola signed Michael Jackson to Sony and released Jackson's album Invincible. Album sales were disappointing, which Jackson blamed on a lack of promotion by Sony. This led Jackson to publicly state that Mottola frequently used racist language and didn't promote the releases by his minority artists. Jackson decided to wait out his contract with Sony but soon discovered that he was obligated to Sony for a much longer period than he had known. It emerged that the lawyer who helped Jackson negotiate the deal with Sony was also working for Sony. Another charge against Mottola in his dealings with Jackson was that he set Invincible up to fail in hopes of putting Jackson in a position financially where he would have no choice but to sell his back catalogue to Sony."

"The behind the scenes wrangling led Jackson to famously refer to Mottola as "very, very, very devilish". (25)

But then many say Michael's concept of Tommy Mattola is completely wrong. That was not surprising since it was very hard to figure out who really cared about Michael and who did not. I am sure it was a huge dilemma for him all of his adult life.

Who then told Michael how long his contract was for? Remember that this is the same thing that happened in the months before he died that caused him to have to do fifty shows instead of ten and work so hard while too old and sick. Who then is the real bad guy? Notice the lawyer's name is not mentioned here. Could lawyers who told Michael the contract said one thing when it really said another be Gatekeepers?

The Entertainment business consists of so, so many players including agents, attorneys, publicists, choreographers, costume people, designer people, photographers, businessmen. There are just so many. None of them wore name tags that said I am also a Gatekeeper.

Michael had no idea who was on his side and who was not. He had no idea who sold his pictures or information to the tabloids. He had no idea who would interview him and turn on him as Bashir did. No one could know. There were too many and they were good at their jobs and in their positions.

The difference between the Handlers and the Gatekeepers is that the Handlers would not have hurt Michael in order to keep the secret that he was really a child or they wouldn't have hurt him much. And I believe that most really liked him if not loved him.

The Gatekeepers were playing for big money and to drown Michael the kid to save Michael the icon would have been their job.

Who the Handlers were as opposed to the Gatekeepers, I am not completely sure. I can't put a name on all of them but I have suspicions of who some of them were and that suspicion came inadvertently from the words of Michael Jackson.

It is not the purpose of condemning them in this book. It is the purpose of this book to let you know they were real and Michael was not crazy. They will one day themselves have to face God and Michael.

I can understand Michael's paranoia and say that it was for sure real. He was and still is a cash cow and how do you know who would kill you for the beef when the milk ran out.

Chapter 12

Begging To Be Heard

"I have all of this...yet I have nothing. The things I really want in my life are the things I don't have. The only thing that matters in life is having someone who understands you, who trusts you and will be with you when you grow old, no matter what." Michael Jackson sitting in a tree at Neverland

So many times Michael told us his plight and so many times we didn't hear him. Like the time he told Barbara Walters that he felt like spaghetti when the fans ripped and pulled at him. Did the fans hear him? Did they care? No.

Michael was a very social person who wanted so much to show us his life. He wanted to join us. He wanted to be part of us. He wanted us to be a part of him.

For those who don't know, Michael contacted a supposed journalist named Martin Bashir to do a video of him at his home. No holds barred, Michael wanted to show the world his beautiful children and Neverland. Martin Bashir turned the tables on him and did so much damage that he seemed like a crazy person and a person dangerous to children. It was after the Bashir tape that a teacher, not the accuser's parent, called authorities to report Michael a possible child molester.

Michael had been taping behind Bashir and did a second program with Maury Povich called "The Footage You Were Never Meant To See" to counter the one by Bashir showing Bashir telling Michael how great he was and how beautiful his children were then turning the tables to call him the opposite. It was said that it was this taping that ultimately lead Michael to be investigated and charged with child molestation and to leave Neverland forever.

The reason Martin Bashir was able to do that horrible documentary was because Michael wanted to let us in. He wanted people to know him and his family. Right brain people are "people" people by nature.

I can say with absolute certainty that Michael tried everything to figure out what was wrong. He tried different religions or befriended those of different religions to try to understand. He connected with Gurus and spiritual people and all sorts of beings. He tried everything not only for his health problems but for his understanding of why he was different and why he was lonely. He tried everything even when it made the papers and made him look bad.

Over and over I would read from various books and articles and see things on YouTube that showed Michael fall down then get up and try again. Maybe a new religion, maybe a new drug, herbal teas from his health nurse, maybe this maybe that. Nothing worked.

Of course, he never could have figured it out on his own because the part of the brain that would figure it out was the part he could not use.

Interview with Barbra Walters:

Michael: "Wacko Jacko. Where did that come from, huh? An English tabloid. I have a heart and I have feelings. I feel that when you do that to me. It's not nice. Don't do it. I'm not a wacko."

Barbara: "There are those who would say that you ask for the attention".

Michael: "No. I don't. The masks, the mysterious behavior. There is not mysterious behavior. No. There's a time when I give a concert ...the people want to come enjoy the show. The star needs some space. He has a heart. He's human." (26)

Did he try to tell us in songs?

Michael wrote a song called "They don't care about us". There are so many possibilities that he could be referring to. Could it be the fans yelling his name over and over so he can't even sit at a dinner place to eat with his family? They certainly didn't care about him in those moments. Or the Tabloids? For sure. So many it seemed didn't care about them.

Today in the news, singer Morrissey returned to the stage only to be hit in the head by a FAN who threw a bottle at him. He walked off the stage. His FANS burst into chants of Morrissey, Morrissey" hoping that he would come back on stage.

"Leave me alone" was to the critics. Michael tried to tell people even in his songs.

"Stop pressuring me. Stop pressuring me." 1995 song from Scream.

Referring to the kids in an interview; "I want them to have some space where they can go to school. I don't want them to be called Wacko Jacko. That's not nice. They call the father that. That isn't nice, right?"

He said the song that that had the lyrics, "kick me, kike me. Don't you black and white me". ...really was about prejudice..."I'm "color blind". They doubted him because sometimes he said things against

95

Jews or blacks. He was angry, he was influenced. He was eight years old. And this *was* about just what he said. I had to laugh when they totally missed the idea that he put "kick me" on the same line as "kike me". He did that because to use such verbiage as "kike" is to injure as a kick is to injure. It was of love, it was about judgment and prejudice. That song makes perfect sense to me.

"Leave it to Michael to have a huge statue of himself towed down the Thames as a publicity stunt. He also had huge statues of him and unveiled in cities in Europe." NOT TRUE! Those statues were of the icon that people adored. They were not Michael. He knew the difference between the show and himself. It was everyone else who didn't.

In Berry Gordy's house Michael saw a picture on the wall of Berry in the outfit of Napoleon Bonaparte. When Michael used the same concept in pictures at his house, with scenes or costumes like the military outfit in his video he was condemned.

He was begging to be heard but each time rejected, rejected, rejected.

Michael was considered to be acting like a spoiled kid when he could not have his way. In reality, what he was asking for and in many cases begging for was what he needed, not what he wanted.

In a letter Michael wrote he said, "Animals strike not from malice, but they want to live. It is the same with those who criticize. They desire our blood, not our pain. This phrase completely confused Frank Deleo and another associate causing them to say he is "losing it". But it made perfect sense to me. He was simply saying they don't intend to hurt me but they are hurting me. What was the confusion? (27)

Michael entered Charter rehabilitation center but after a short stay he simply wanted to get out. He was older now and had enough experience to know right away if the people around him were going to understand him and really be able to help him. Or should I say he would know pretty quickly that those he was with didn't have a clue about what was going on with him. It wasn't that he was not trying. He knew it was hopeless.

In the book by Tamborelli it was written, "He would often start casual relationships with people, many of whom were certain that their relationship would grow, only to find out that Michael had left them behind." Not true, either. He started relationships because he wanted to be close to people. He left them behind because he could not fit with them. (28)

As time went on the plot thickened, the child became more trapped, and the pleas to be freed and understood were echoed more and more until they were silenced. What did he say then? The boy who would not curse in public? What did he say when he was told a lawyer wanted to take his kids? "Tell her to go to hell." The boy had grown.

So, all the things that Michael said about himself were true when he told us about himself and told the best he could. Every thing that he tried to convey about himself was real. He tried to tell us. He begged for help. We couldn't hear. We wouldn't hear. We didn't hear.

Chapter 13

Desperation

...have mercy on me for I've been bleeding for a long time now."
Michael Jackson

I want you to imagine the world Michael lived in. I will tell it to you the best I can as if I were him.

"What a bright place the world was when I was safe with my thoughts. Until the day the light went out. Something was gone. I could still sing and dance as I had always done. I could draw and joke but I could not think. Something was missing and that something was a piece of me.

I wasn't completely gone because I knew it was once there. I was still there but simply didn't work. I remember it and I really miss it. Well, I think I remember it.

In just one day, one moment, I became Peter Pan. Others were no longer connected to me. My brother, almost my age, was now so much older. I was foreign, alien, distant. It made me feel alone, and isolated. I knew it. I could feel it. But I couldn't understand it. Each day was so lonely.

As time went on it got worse as of course it should. We are social beings and I am very social. All the people were encased in glass, untouchable, unreachable. But I needed them. If only they had no mind, just like me. Then we could be together. I miss them so much. "Every day is a search for that which I cannot find."

In Rabbi Shmuley Boteach's book *The Michael Jackson Tapes,* Michael says, "I felt I needed someone. I was too shy to be around real people…I didn't talk to them (manikins), it wasn't like old ladies talking to plants. I always thought about…Why do I have these? I love them, it's like real babies, kids, people but it makes me feel like I am in a room with people."

Does this sound familiar to anyone? Remember "Wilson"? Remember the volleyball that Tom Hanks risked his life to save from floating away in "Castaway". We thought nothing of his attachment to a volleyball. We thought nothing of him talking to that volleyball and holding on to it for dear life. To Michael, those manikins were "Wilson".

That volleyball had nothing in common with people except that it looked a bit like a person. We understood why Tom Hanks would use a volleyball, it was simple. There were no people around to talk to.

On that same note, there were no people for Michael to talk to either. There were no people who were like him. Grownups were too capable. Children grew up. He was as unable to communicate with people around him due to his disablility, as Tom Hanks was unable to communicate with adults due to distance. Both had a barrier. Both were "painfully lonely".

"I used to be lonely painfully lonely… you have no idea. I used to walk the streets looking for people to talk to." Michael Jackson

Despite the resurgence in sales, he complained of feeling alone -- almost abandoned. He was twenty three.

"One of the loneliest people in the world."

"Everything seems to be foreign to me or new and I'm just now beginning to enjoy friendship, which is new for me." Michael Jackson

This was interesting. I had come to realize that though he had friends like Brooke Shields it was Emmanuel Lewis he called his best friend.

Emmanuel was still a kid and he looked like a kid. Emmanuel was Michael's first real friend. Remember, he worked constantly and had no relationships, especially those his psychological age until Emmanuel came along and seemingly to Michael fit the bill, at least for a little while.

When I would watch videos and interviews of Michael it was clear that he was always reaching to find the answer that would free him. Always eye to eye explaining, and waiting for a connection. All along he was trying to make sense of it himself. He knew he wasn't crazy. He made complete sense to him and I have to say now he makes complete sense to me too.

He knew he wasn't gay considering that he did not prefer to hang out with adults and certainly not male adults. He knew he wasn't a pedophile because he knew he would never hurt a child.

Of the animatronic ET Michael said, 'He was so real that I was talking to him." I kissed him before I left. The next day I missed him." (28)

It was this statement that made me understand one reason for the closeness Michael needed to have with children. The loneliness was so deep and deeper than for most because he was so right brain active meaning he really loved everyone.

There were four parts to Michael.

101

Part one was the entertainer which included all things right brain. I am very happy to say that we really would have been able to have the right brain Michael entertainer we have. We would have had the Entertainer that we had come to know and love. His desire to sing and his ability was there long before the impairment began to take away from him. His talent would have gone on with or without the left brain damage. I am happy for that because I really liked his music and dancing and, after writing this book, have come to really love it. I am also happy to say that this part of Michael was his correct age. This part did not suffer and grew as Michael grew. On stage, for the most part we were seeing the adult entertainer, the real person.

The second part of Michael was the Michael from birth to eight or so years of age. This is the Michael we saw at Neverland. Michael would say he was at home on stage and he was at home at Neverland. This is the Michael coupled with the right brain that we saw in the Barbara Walters interview say, "chick, ding". If you were visiting Michael's family with him as a normal adult this is the Michael his mother would be talking about in his past. Michael did this and Michael did that and Michael loved water guns and would play practical jokes on everyone. He got in a lot of trouble. This is the child that all of our families could talk about as we got older.

The fourth part of Michael is the part we and he never got to see. It was the part that would have been the grown up. It is the part that would have had a family, had a religion, chosen a house that was two stories or one story. He would have argued political things and maybe been the guy who could beat anyone at poker. This was the grown up Michael that the third part of Michael was always striving to meet. This was the Michael the third part of Michael existed to search for and find. This is the Michael that the injury kept from coming out.

Now for the third part of Michael. This part is what I call "desperation". This is the part of Michael that got him in trouble. This is the part that tried to find the fourth part of Michael so he could be whole. This is the part of Michael you see contemplating in some pictures and videos. This is the part of Michael you see pleading for answers in interviews and picking the person's brain. This is the part that picked the brains of people like Rabbi Shmuley Boteach and this is the part that attached to children so he could find who he was. Remember, attaching to children is a normal growing process. It is what all children naturally do. This part would not have existed if there was no injury.

Of course, he didn't know why he was so attracted to the concept of hanging out with children. That would have taken left brain logic which he didn't have. Remember the "hole in the bucket", the perpetual trap.

Every odd thing you saw Michael do was due to either his lack of logic or his quiet desperate attempt to find out who he was…to grow. There was not one action that I saw that was done to hurt anyone. I can't stress that enough.

"I'm so miserable. I'm having a terrible life."

The reason I cried so much when I learned the situation with Michael was because I knew instantly the depth of the deep dark hole in which he lived. When he said he was all alone in the world I knew what he meant. I decided there was no way I could put into words what it was like for him so I thought you should live it and then hear it from Michael.

When I was in college I took a class to learn to teach the blind. We were made to walk around with blindfolds and being lead by another. After the exercise the teacher said something so true. She said that we could never really understand because we knew that we could take the blindfolds off any time. Remember that when walking through this exercise with me.

Here is your exercise: You are going to walk in Michael's shoes. He was forced to live in your world so for this you will live in his. You will have be as talented as he was so you will be a physicist. As Michael was forced to live in an adult world in which he did not fit, you will live in a child's world in which you do not fit. For one day you will watch cartoons all day. You will go to work like right brain Michael did during the day as a child game tester then you need to spend the rest of the day watching cartoons. Are you bored? Now do it for a week. Now do it for a month. Are you bored and lonely? Are your friends saying they have to be somewhere else? Would you be begging for freedom like Michael did? Now do it for a year. Now you need to realize that the blindfold will never leave and you have to watch cartoons for the rest of your life.

Michael was forced to live in a world that was "foreign" just as you did in the exercise only for him it was forever. "I'm having a terrible life."

'People hurt each other over and over and over again. I spend a lot of time being sad. I feel like I'm in a well. And no one can reach me". (29)

I am not comfortable around "normal people".

Michael cried so much at She's out of my life that they left the tears in.

"Can you help me?"

"I'm so miserable. I'm having a terrible life."

"It was as if he was an alien just visiting from another world."

'Why does everyone else get to be happy, and I'm always thrashing through the mud?' (30)

Once Michael had to go to a reception. He was told there would be children there. When he stepped in there were tons of adults but no children. He refused to go unless the children arrived. How boring the evening would be with a ton of adults and no kids for an eight year old boy.

At age 26 they wanted Michael to write his memoirs. He said, I'm still trying to figure it all out myself." [31] Little did he know that he would try his whole life, never get there and nearly go to prison trying.

"People don't know what it's like for me. No one knows, really. No one should judge what I've done with my life, not unless they've been in my shoes every horrible day and every sleepless night."

"How can I get past this pain?"

Chapter 14

Caged

Albert Einstein: Everyone should be respected as an individual, but no one idolized.

"I'm running for my life." Michael Jackson

"You feel like you're spaghetti among thousands of hands. They're just ripping and pulling your hair. And you feel that any moment you're gonna break" Michael Jackson

It began in May 1970 when the Jackson 5 were mobbed by 3500 screaming fans. Security and police prevented them from being completely overwhelmed. Michael was eleven years old. He was scared to death.

When Michael was on stage and said, "Here it is, the tune that knocked The Beatles out of number one." The crowd went wild. Row after row in the audience toppled over and people were falling over themselves to get to them. [32]

Diana Ross once warned Michael that people in show business can get hurt.

...Afterwards as the limo pulled away, fans hurled themselves at its windows.

In 1971 the boys were playing at Madison Square Garden in New York when after only two minutes of playing the audience stormed the stage and they had to be extracted. When the show ended they had to be quickly lead to their limousines but did not finish their last song. The audience went crazy when they realized they were gone and pushed past security to search for them. [33]

"I've been running for my life like that, you can't go that way 'cause they're over there... and I said hold on, stop. This person deserves their privacy. You are not allowed to go there. I've been around the world running, hiding." Michael Jackson

In 1971 fans started to chant "Michael, Michael, Michael". When they opened the door fans burst in and started kissing and hugging Michael. [33]

"Large plugs of hair were jerked from the scalp under Jermaine's giant Afro by souvenir hunters...Tito was bruised and shaken by the stampede of the thundering herd....Michael was almost choked to death...They were pulling both ends of his scarf, actually choking him...He recalls having to run through screaming girls with his eyes covered by his hands for fear that their nails would scratch him..."You feel as if you're going to suffocate or be dismembered." [34]

...A nine year old threatened to use a knife on a hotel doorman unless he allowed her access to Michael's room.

...the Rolls-Royce limousine carrying the group sustained twelve thousand dollars worth of damage when it was dented and scratched by young girls clawing to get to their idols.

... souvenir hunters stripped their limousine of its cushions, radio, lights...it was this way whenever the brothers traveled for the rest of their tour, whether in Amsterdam, Brussels, Munich, Frankfurt or Paris."

At age 19, "Michael had to escape to the roof of a Woolco department store when ten thousand people caused a riot...where Michael promised to sign autographs."

"Once at a record store in San Francisco, over a thousand kids showed up. They pushed forward and broke a window. A big piece of glass fell on a girl. And the girl's throat was slit." [35]

"They don't think you're real. Once a fan asked me the most embarrassing question and in front of everyone. She said, "Do you go to the bathroom?"

Rabbi Shmuley Boteach says, "You get chills listening to this. His celebrity had created a degree of isolation, where he could not simply feel comfortable around other people - he felt that everybody wanted something from him; he felt that he was trapped in this cocoon of fame." [36]

"I can't go out there. They'll get me for sure. They're around the corner and they want to get their hands on me" Michael said of going out to eat. "The terror in his eyes seemed genuine." You can see here that the reporter that asked him out didn't believe how bad it was. Neither did I until I wrote this book. [37]

Michael lived in a prison. Sadly, his children lived in that prison with him. When I first saw it, I was dumbfounded. Tabloid people screamed his name as he walked to what may have been his death in prison and fans pulled at him wanting to touch him no matter the cost to him. No wonder he wore a mask. He should have worn a suit of armor.

"A thousand hands" is what it really looked like when I actually saw the mob attacking Michael. "Ripping" "Pulling" "Break" "Running for my life" They were surely the right words. People surrounded Michael for yards in every direction. He was encircled by people who would rip at him and pull at him and would not care if he broke as long as they got to touch Michael Jackson.

They yelled "Michael" as if they were his friends as they tried to grab at him. The people were in a frenzy. It was complete chaos...mob rule. People were reaching, sweating, grabbing and crying. It was sick and it happened all the time. And they called *him* "Wacko".

Imagine no matter where you go, no matter how hard you tried to hide you have people screaming and grabbing at you and taking your picture. Everywhere... everywhere in the entire world.

I always wondered why movie stars had to have such big houses. It seemed pretentious to me. Not that I thought about it much. I have to say that now I understand. I can tell you that when someone tells me they want to be a movie star I think, "What a hard life you may live." I wonder if the stars had it to do all over again if they would have taken a different path.

Michael often said he would love to just go to a grocery store. His friends took him once. It was a fiasco. What he was really saying was that he wanted to live a normal life. He wanted to go to a store and buy things that he could shop for in the store. He wanted to walk the streets like the rest of us. Whenever I go to the grocery store now I feel oddly grateful for the opportunity to do such a mundane thing.

Tabloids:

This is an interview done by Larry King with Macaulay Culkin. The topic is tabloids. [38]

KING: How many lies have you read about you in the tabloids?

CULKIN: Millions. Yes. I mean, forget about it. It just comes with the territory. I remember I got a call from my lawyer one day. Calls me up and goes, Hey Mac, are you there? I go, of course, I'm here. I just checking because I just got a call from CNN that you died of a drug overdose?

And I go, no, I'm still here, but thanks a lot, thanks for calling, talk to you tomorrow. It was so just surreal, you know it was just one of these things. It's like a cliché.

KING: There are people 50-years-old that can't handle that.

CULKIN: At that time, especially because I was taking a step back and I wasn't working, everything, you know, like when I quit, I just basically said you can have it. You can have the Macaulay Culkin. You can have that image and you can control it and you can say whatever you want with it, my mom or my dad or the newspapers, whatever, because I didn't care. It wasn't mine and I was never going to do this again. I was never planning on acting or going into this ever again. So, that's why I really didn't care. So, I never hired a publicist to like protect me or anything."

I remember reading where Michael stopped to look in a mirror when passing by. Oh my God. So, what? He was labeled as vain by the reporter who was there at the time. How totally wrong that was if you knew anything about Michael. Vanity was never part of his life, at all. I wish it had been. But here he was labeled. Until doing this book I never knew how little he was heard. Except for a few friends who listened he was screaming on the moon.

Paparazzi:

In Michael's interview with Barbra Walters he told us of the time he was in the stall in the bathroom and suddenly he saw the camera come under the stall. "Chick, chick, chick, chick, chick, chick, chick, chick. Oh my God". Those were his words. [39]

I hope you take the time to Google on YouTube the words "Michael Jackson Mobbed" and see what it was really like for Michael and his children. Please do so.

I remember seeing on the news a long time ago when Paul Newman was at a restaurant and a person came up to him in the middle of his meal with his family and said, "Can I have your autograph?" He said, "I am eating dinner with my family." I remember that from so long ago because at first I thought it a bit rude and then realized that it was the fan who was being rude. Little did I know that years later I would be rummaging through the horrible situation that the stars live in and wondering how Paul Newman didn't slug that person.

The situation was horrible, really horrible. I had no idea how bad it was. They were paid tens of thousands of dollars to take the picture of an eight year old boy. Why not? They were paid as much to take a picture of Tom Cruise's baby and Brad Pitt's babies. How sad are we?

Debbie Rowe "I didn't think it was going to be this brutal." [40]

The Fans:

"The name "fan" is short for fanatic. Touring with Michael Jackson, we got no sleep 'cause all night, the all night vigils chanting Michael Jackson all night, all day. It was like the second coming." Siedah Garrett [41]

Michael lived in a prison made by people who professed to care about him and professed to "love" him. He was unable to go outside his home without being mobbed.

From the News:

"The controversial singer was mobbed by fans at the world-famous attraction when he arrived with his three children last night. Jackson left Madam Tussaud's after spending over an hour touring the attraction's famous wax statues."

From the News:
Police had been drafted in to control the crowds during his exit but his people-carrier was mobbed by fans who screamed and chanted his name.

They prevented the star from leaving as they surrounded the vehicle and brought traffic chaos for a few minutes to the Marylebone Road in central London. When it finally pulled away large numbers chased after the singer." [42] [43]

From the News:
LONDON, UNITED KINGDOM, Friday, March 6, 2009. "Michael Jackson arrives with his kids to see Oliver! starring Rowan Atkinson at the Theatre Royal, Drury Lane. Crowds swarm around Michael Jackson in a moment of mass hysteria. Michael is ushered swiftly into the theatre, as fans scream his name flooded around the foyer." [44]

From the news: Michael Jackson was mobbed by fans during an LA shopping trip. Michael Jackson was mobbed by fans as he took his children on a shopping trip in Los Angeles." [45]

From the News: "Masked Michael Jackson was mobbed by fans as he tried to sneak out the back door of a hospital."

From the News: "Not fond of public appearances as of late, Michael Jackson was mobbed by fans as he tried to sneak out the back door of a medical building in Beverly Hills on Wednesday (January 14)."

From the News: "Singer Michael Jackson was mobbed by fans at London waxworks museum Madame Tussauds during a stay in the capital."

113

The crowd gathered and began to yell. You can see it on YouTube. This took place where Michael was trying to eat dinner:

"We want Michael. We want Michael. We want Michael. We want Michael. We want Michael. We want Michael. We want Michael. We want Michael. We want Michael". It's even annoying seeing it written here. 10 plus screams Then again 8. "We want Michael. We want Michael. We want Michael. We want Michael. We want Michael. We want Michael. We want Michael. We want Michael. We want Michael. We want Michael." Ah yes, and a family with child in tow... chanting as all the others with dad the person who is supposed to be the strong one right there too. (46)

And all this chaos because Michael wanted to eat in a public place. We should have wished on him...eat in peace. His name was yelled 56 times plus screams in the video alone. It could have been hundreds of times for all we knew.

Michael Jackson is inside so let's everyone sing a song that he did and disrupt his dinner. Wow, we really love him. Let's get everyone walking by to join us. Aren't we great? Michael come out and put down your fork no matter how hungry you are and say "Hi" to us selfish ones... the ones yelling "We love you, Michael".

What you want? What you want! Maybe what Michael wanted was to eat dinner in peace. Doing appearances and dancing is work for him. That was his JOB.

When Cher was asked about where she was going on the way to her performance she said, "I'm going to work. I'm going to work." Here they all were yelling that Michael should get up from dinner and go to work.

The fans who were supposed to love Michael would chant his name day and night. Where were the police? Isn't that illegal? If an ex-husband stood outside his ex-wife's house yelling her name over and over he would be arrested. I guess that is why Michael said he had no rights.

This was the best one of all. "Michael Jackson's casket was mobbed by fans."

Michael:

Michael himself was responsible for some of the problem. He would often encourage the paparazzi response and the fan response by giving them what they were after. Why did he do that? Because he was a logically disabled eight year old boy. So in reality, it was not Michael who was responsible for the problem along with others but his disability.

From the News: Masked Michael Jackson was mobbed by fans as he tried to sneak out the back door of a hospital. (47)

The disability: Wacko Jacko stopped to sign autographs for his adoring fans before hopping into his car with a packet of Kettle Chips to snack on for the journey. (48)

From the News: "Singer Michael Jackson was mobbed by fans at London waxworks museum Madame Tussauds during a stay in the capital."

The disability: "On Friday Jackson signed autographs after being pursued by fans through an underground car park near a recording studio."

The disability: The star has also been spotted in the Dorchester Hotel, London, meeting fans and posing for photographs. (49)

From the News: Not fond of public appearances as of late, Michael Jackson was mobbed by fans as he tried to sneak out the back door of a medical building in Beverly Hills on Wednesday (January 14).

The disability: Despite blocking his remodeled mug from being seen, Jackson did take a few moments to sign autographs for his adoring fans before hopping into his car.

Barbara Walters: "Though they told no one they were going to be at the hotel there were paparazzi swarming."

The disability:

If you look at this video you will see Michael, though he was found out and just spoke of the paparazzi and fans swarming him, waving to the people.

Inside people:

I saw a video of Michael where he said he was going for a rare drive with friends. You could see him doing a little dance type of thing in the back seat. Then it dawned on me that there was a camera mounted in the car. Was it for security? It was not a flattering video I have to say. The big question is: How did it get on the internet?

Someone in his immediate entourage had to have given the tape to someone to put it on YouTube. But who? Who had access to the camera in the car? Was it a close friend? Security? The video was so unflattering that I will not post where I saw it here but why would someone post it for all to see? Certainly that person would not be a friend.

Most of this book was taken from videos on YouTube. The camera showed a gaunt terrified Michael as he was escorted into the courtroom. Wait a minute, the camera? I now noticed cameras everywhere. I mean everywhere. Nowhere could he turn without a camera in his face. There as he entered the courtroom was a man with a camera in his face. How did he get there and who let him in? Who let him in? Who...let...him...in?

Was Michael paranoid or did he just wonder how those cameras got in places they shouldn't have been? Oh, and don't forget, they were at his "private" funeral. Even Elizabeth Taylor was said to be shocked at that.

As time went on I began to ask...who brought the camera? Who allowed that person in? Who sold it to the media? Were there insiders who were not his friends? I have no doubt.

Crazy world:

In Gabon, Michael touched his nose on one trip and the public thought he was indicating they smell as that was what it meant in their culture. This caused a national disaster. He had to leave the country.

What???

Here you have a person who had an itch and has to leave the country because he scratched it. Is this the same boy who was honored all over the world from royalty for his humanitarian work? How confusing it must have all been for a left brain disabled person who was eight years old. How confusing it is to me!

Tabloids were chasing him. Fans professing to love him pulled at him so he had to run for his life. Insiders sold his pictures to the media. The world he lived in was crazy and on top of that he had to deal with his own disabilities. Would you need antidepressants after all this? I probably would have.

Michael was a great businessman, Michael didn't care about money, Michael was sick, Michael was healthy, Michael wanted to do the concerts, Michael didn't want to do the concerts, Michael was

eccentric, Michael was magic, Michael was smart, Michael was misguided, Michael was vain and always looked in the mirror, Michael hated how he looked. Michael was weird, Michael was a genius, Michael had a gay lover, Michael had two gay lovers, Michael had a secret girlfriend, Michael secretly married his children's nanny, Michael was undergoing a sex change, Michael tried to buy the bones of the Elephant Man, Michael didn't try to buy the bones of the Elephant Man but told the tabloids he did, Michael slept in a hyperbaric chamber to stay young (hey, I would have done that), Michael has a nose, Michael doesn't have a nose, Michael is a recluse, named himself the King of Pop, Michael was named by Elizabeth Taylor the King of Pop, Michael didn't want to be black, Michael was proud to be black, Michael is loving, kind, humble and a child molester (same person stating this), Michael was vicious, Michael was bathing in animal blood, Michael only cared about himself, …
now here is a new concept they wouldn't want to mull around. Michael Jackson was…8…years…old.

I have gotten a real glimpse of the crazy world stars live in and can honestly say that I would rather live in a box under a bridge than have their wealthy imprisoned life. And the trap is worldwide.

"People don't know what it's like for me. No one knows, really. No one should judge what I've done with my life, not unless they've been in my shoes every horrible day and every sleepless night."

Chapter 15

Really Michael

Albert Einstein: Logic will get you from A to B. Imagination will take you everywhere.

The phenomenon that was Michael Jackson was due to three things: his extraordinary talent as a performer, his personality and his heart. People loved him as a child when he burst on the scene years ago and later they loved him for his heart and his personality. They liked him as a person and performer. If his look hadn't changed because of his disease and he hadn't had children sleeping in his bed he would have gone on as an icon for his entire life.

Michael would have been able to be childlike and been accepted as such with nearly no problems. Neverland would have been accepted and he would have been seen as a person who just loved children and wanted to do good things.

But the eight year old boy kept fighting to come out. And rightfully so. What Michael's life should have been was the eight year old boy with the talent. What it became was the talent interrupted by the eight year old boy.

People who met Michael liked him as Oprah did. "I liked him. I really, really, really liked him."

John Landis, director of Thriller said, "Everyone who worked with Mike, liked him." Why wouldn't we? He was fun, he was funny, he was talented, he was loving and he was genuinely interested in…you.

Michael was a fixer of problems that hurt people. Michael was a talented beyond belief dancer. Michael was a talented, beyond belief, singer. Michael was a great father. Michael was a great friend. . Michael was fun. Michael was funny. Michael was a great, great entertainer. Michael was a wonderful man. And Michael was a left brain damaged eight year old boy.

I'm sure it wasn't easy seeing dying and sick children for a person so sensitive or for any person for that matter. He may have gone to those places because it was part of his job but even if that was the reason he loved them when he got there. That was Michael. That was the same Michael Jackson who wiped off the dancer who fell in the dirt. With all the charities Michael gave to and all the hospitals he visited what showed me the real Michael was the dancer who fell in the dirt. That was Michael the automatically loving being.

I disagree with Jermaine in his song and the statement he made about Michael and I have to address it. The statement included the words "You say you're a man, but that you'll never be." The question is what is a man? One definition from Merriam Webster is as follows: "one possessing in high degree the qualities considered distinctive of manhood." I can tell you what a man is to me. As I see beings of the male persuasion walking around I have to question how many of them are really men. The burly man who walks by dodging child support payments he doesn't want to pay, the man on the television who was convicted of killing the mother of his children because he couldn't have his girlfriend if they were around. The beggar on the corner.

A man, to me, is a male being who takes care of himself financially and leans on himself. A man is a person who is male and takes care of his family. A man is a male who cares for the world in which he lives. I would have to say that no matter how much the left brain logic interfered with Michael's life. He was, for all intents and purposes that really matter, a man in my vision.

Of Michael's talent Sheryl Crow said, "He has a resonance that goes on forever. He's so bright and so clear sounding. The fact that he dances while he's singing that, to me, is amazing." Greg Phillinganes said, "He's got pipes of plutonium. "When he sang it he looked like he lived it." Berry Gordy

Of his heart I can only say, "Beautiful." Caretaking of the world, loving the world is a right brain action. Knowing that you can't save everyone is a left brain action. Michael thought he could save the world and surely wanted to and tried to. In my research the giving was enormous. I really mean enormous. He wanted to save the world and when he saw something that was not right he wanted to fix it. And he really did make them pick up a bug from the stage so he didn't step on it! How funny is that? (50)

Michael was an adult and an eight year old boy with left brain logic impairment who was stuck in a man's body and a man's career.

I am happy to say, Michael was not always a sad person. He actually had a fun life, as lives go. It was dangerous as Steven Spielberg indicated when he called him a "fawn in a burning forest". But, he had a lot of fun too. The reason he seemed so sad, was because he was so desperately looking for an answer from everyone he met. At times you could see him contemplating, or attempting to contemplate, in the hope that he could figure out what was wrong. You see him deep in thought only to be stopped by this impairment. An impairment he had no clue he had.

The friends he had, the people he knew:

Since I didn't pay very much attention to Michael in his life, I didn't know much about it. I was surprised, in fact, a bit shocked when I saw some of the people in his life and some of the people who were close to him. It was hard to decipher who was really close to him and who was just an acquaintance but one thing is certain, many people really liked Michael. When I think of Michael I can see why they liked him.

Here are a few names that surprised me. I know there are more.

Gregory Peck: Michael Jackson was friends with Gregory Peck! What an unlikely pair. On the Internet you can see Gregory Peck getting off one of Michael's rides vowing never to ride that one again. Michael thought it was really funny. It was the Zipper! Michael assisted in Mr. Peck's funeral helping his wife who also used to ride Michael's Neverland rides and visit with him. Gregory Peck complimented Michael on the raising of his beautiful children. I was stunned to see that they knew each other and that Gregory Peck was his friend. Imagine, Atticus and Michael!

Lou Ferrigno: He was considered Michael's long time close friend and trainer. They knew each other for fifteen years. (51)

Marlon Brando was considered a long time close friend to Michael and often would spend time at his Neverland ranch. He would at times use it as a retreat. (52)

President Ronald Reagan and Nance Reagan: In 1984 President Reagan invited Michael to the White House to receive an award. The Presidential Public Safety Communication Award was given to Michael for his support of charities that helped people overcome alcohol and drug abuse. President Reagan's speech contained comments like "Well, isn't this a thriller?" As you will read in this book it is not my belief that Michael was addicted to drugs in any way so the next statement form the President is completely accurate.

"Michael Jackson is proof of what a person can accomplish through a lifestyle free of alcohol or drug abuse. People young and old can respect that, And if Americans follow his example, then we can face up to the problem of drinking and driving, and we can, in Michael's words, *Beat It.* They sent him a letter saying they were happy he was not too hurt from the Pepsi commercial. [53]

Elton John: Elton John was in the middle of a "White Tie and Tiara Ball" when he heard of the loss of Michael. He had been long time friends and worked on things concerning AIDS together. He dedicated the song "Don't Let the Sun Go Down on Me" to Michael.

Paul McCartney: Paul McCartney hung out with Michael and worked with Michael on music.

Dave Dave: formerly called by a name he no longer uses and out of respect for his wishes, neither will I. He was a burn victim when he was six years old and anyone who is my age will remember the tragic cruelty of a grown man who did not have the courage to do to himself what he did to his son. Dave was burned on most of his body. He was a friend of Michael's and I am sure as Michael was "color blind" he was "burn blind" also. Dave said "Michael Jackson was like a Father to me."

Ryan White: Michael sang the song "Gone Too Soon" for Ryan White who lost his battle with AIDS of which he was diagnosed at the age of 13 when he received a contaminated transfusion. Ryan's mother stated that Neverland was "a place between heaven and earth". "He didn't care what race you were, what color you were, what was your handicap, what was your disease. He just loved children."

Katherine Hepburn: At the 1984 Grammys the audience wanted Michael to take off his sunglasses. He said something to the effect of "My friend Katherine Hepburn said I should take them off so this is for her." She and Michael were reported to be pen pals.

Oona Chaplin: "Oona's old friend Sophia Loren, "something of a Jackson groupie." had been attending Jackson's concerts, and when the singer came to Switzerland the Italian actress did arrange for them to meet. He (Michael Jackson) went to the Manoir and was given the tour of the estate by Oona. At one point she told him that he and Charlie "had a lot in common: you were born poor and had to strive to achieve all that you have." (54)

Lillian Disney: She would call him on the set as well as visit him.

Fred Astaire: It was reported that he also visited Michael on the set. He spoke of him as a friend and complimented him on his dancing.

Here are other people he met or knew in his life:

Bill Cosby, Princess Diana, Queen Elizabeth II, Donald Trump, Marla Maples, Clint Eastwood, Wayne Dyer, Jimmy Carter, Henry Fonda (took him fishing), The Fonda Family, Neil Austrian, Little Richard, President Bush, Liza Minnelli (he accompanied her to her fathers funeral), Lionel Richie, Jeanie White, Sammy Davis Jr. (from whom he would borrow movies to learn dance steps), Michael Eisner, Smoky Robinson, Diana Ross, Steven Spielberg, David Geffen, Quincy Jones, Sean Lennon, James Brown, Eddie Murphy, Deandra Douglas, Angelica Huston, Jane Goodall, Tatum O'Neal, Nelson Mandela, Bill Cosby, Harry Belafonte, Denzel Washington, H. Ross Perot (who took him on his boat), Sheikh Rashid Ahmed, Michael Jordan, Jessie Jackson, Stevie wonder, Muhammad Ali, Spike Lee, Gabon's President Omar Bongo, Benny Hill, Robert E. Johnson, Naomi Campbell, Lou Rawls, Bill Clinton, Hilary Clinton, Chelsea Clinton, Fleetwood Mac, Wesley Snipes, Patti Lavelle, Suzanne de Passe, Gladys Knight, Dick Clark, Lionel Richie, Richard Pryor, Jackie Wilson, George Lucus, Kenny Rogers, John and Carolyn Kennedy, Joan Collins, Johnny Carson, Michael Caine, Kris Kristofferson and so many others.

David Smithy: I am putting the name David Smithy in here to represent all the people all over the world that were helped by Michael and by his organizations. There were way, way too many to mention. I used David because we didn't know him and those were the people Michael cared about most. The people who were not sitting on a pedestal, people just like you and me. David was dying of Cystic Fibrosis and Michael gave him his jacket from Beat It and a black sequenced glove he wore to the American Music Awards. Putting all the names of all the people Michael personally helped would take volumes.

Here are some charities:

YMCA Los Angeles,
Make a Wish Foundation,
Princes Trust,
The United Negro College Fund,
USA,
Boy Scouts,
He paid for funeral of Temptations David Ruffin,
Camp Ronald McDonald,
Juvenile Diabetes,
Minority Aids Foundation,
He paid for funeral arrangements for Ramon Sanchez Jr.,
Americares,
Heal LA,
$100,000.00 raised for Atlanta Children's Foundation in response to children being kidnapped and murdered in Atlanta.
National campaign against teenage drunk driving,
Michael Jackson scholarship
Ronald McDonald Camp for Good Times
TJ Martell Foundation for leukemia and cancer research.
United Support for Artists for Africa
USA Africa,
Elizabeth Taylor AIDS Foundation,
We Are The World, raised over $100 million

Michael donated an estimated $500 million to charity in his lifetime. He visited numerous hospitals all over the world.
AIDS Project LA
American Cancer Society
Angel Food
DreamStreet Kids
Dreams Come True Charity

Michael won an award for the "Most Charities Supported by a Pop Star" in the 2000 edition of the Guinness Book of World Records for supporting 39 charities. At the time he gave most he was at the top of the charts as a musician and icon.

In addition he gave through an auction to organizations like UNESCO

- founded the Heal the World Foundation. Where millions of dollars had been raised which airlifted supplies to Sarajevo and paid for a Hungarian child's desperately needed liver transplant among other things.
-raised money and awareness for HIV/AIDS
- donated his Pepsi settlement of 1.5 million to the Brotman Medical Center in California
- We Are The World charity single raised over $63 million for famine relief
- All proceeds from the single Man in the Mirror went to charity

Michael was an outstanding philanthropist, humanitarian who gave of his time and money as well as his heart.

"The death of Michael Jackson is a great American tragedy. His heart had been battered on all fronts, but he believed in humanity and wanted to change the world." Mel Wilson, Heal the World on the front page of their website.

It should be stated that during Michael's life there were many people who loved him. There were very many women who mothered him.

He spoke of his tutor, Ms. Fine rubbing his hand and comforting him when he was young and there was the loving attention he got from Shirley Temple Black in her warm homey kitchen and of course Elizabeth Taylor, who said she loved him like a son, to name some who were not even family.

Michael the Dad:

Michael felt he was a father to every child especially needy or sick ones. He wanted them to call him Daddy Michael. He wanted to save them all and he wanted to make them all happy. He gave to them of his money, time and heart. Isn't that what a father would do?

The children of the world that Michael helped basically said thank you and were truly grateful but went on with their lives. Some of the children he helped never even met him and he didn't know their names. The children that every day gave back to Michael were those he called his own children. They were really his life. They were everything. Thank God for them.

Many people think it was upsetting to see the children with veils on their heads or masks on their faces. I, on the other hand, thought it was very loving. And that was when I was not paying any attention to Michael. I spoke to a retired policeman in Santa Barbara about the situation for celebrities and the photographers. He said that he once saw a photographer hang from an airplane to take a picture of Brad Pitt's house.

Michael said that he couldn't even go to the bathroom without them trying to take his picture. So, wouldn't a loving parent want to protect a child from such a prison? He kept those children's faces from the public, from me, for over ten years. Michael obviously wanted to show the world the children he was so proud of. That is why he held Blanket out for all to see. He kept them covered for them so that they could hopefully walk the earth in freedom, something he was never able to do. He was mocked, belittled, ridiculed, treated with scorn and

God knows what else in order to give those kids what he did not have. The fact that Michael did this was heroic to me. It was what a loving father in his position would do. I applaud him for it and wish those actions had continued beyond his death. I have to say that I was horrified when they weren't. I was horrified; too, that no one said a thing about that.

"It is as though an unexplainable part within Michael is able to reach children close to death; his touch seems to act as some soothing balm for kids facing a frightening time. It is an important positive side of Michael, and the one he thinks is the best thing about himself." He's not afraid to look into the worst suffering and find the smallest part that is positive and beautiful." Frank Deleo. [55]

Every night the kids would come in on stretchers, so sick they could hardly hold their heads up. Michael would kneel down at the stretchers and put his face down right beside theirs so that he could have his picture taken with them, and then give them a copy so they could remember the moment. I couldn't handle it. I'd be in the bathroom crying. The kids would perk up right in his presence. If it gave them a couple more days' energy, to Michael it was worth it." Seth Riggs, Michael's music teacher. [56]

I would like to make a statement here about the women in Michael's life. Those women would be Debbie Rowe, Elizabeth Taylor and Lisa Presley. The side of Michael in the previous paragraphs was the Michael they saw making them admire and love him. Lisa went on trips all over the world with him watching him love these dying children. In pictures you can see her glowing face as he holds a dying child. That and the Michael who wrote the poem below is the Michael Lisa saw.

In every dealing, every deed
You are there, as the seed
I know now, for I have seen

What could have happened could have been
There is no need to try so hard
For in your sleeve you hold the card
For every fortune, every fame
The Kingdom's here for us to claim
In every fire, every hearth
There's a spark gives new birth

To all those songs never sung
All those longings in hearts still young
Beyond all hearing, beyond all seeing
In the core of your Being
Is a field that spans infinity
Unbounded pure is the embryo of divinity
If we could for one moment BE
In an instant we would see
A world where no one has suffered or toiled
Of pristine beauty never soiled
Of sparkling waters, singing skies
Of hills and valleys where no one dies

(from the poem Quantum Leap by Michael Jackson)

Though I am surrounded with men who would think this is crazy, I have to say that a man who spoke as he did in poetry and spent his time and money flying from country to country giving dying children all over the world happiness and love as Michael did would have my heart in an instant even if he looked like the cross between The Wild Man of Borneo and the Loch Ness Monster.

When it came to Michael and people who needed him these words surely rang true. "Just call my name and I'll be there'.

When I think of Michael these are the words for me that ring true.

"Where there is love, I'll be there."

Chapter 16

Michael Didn't Know

Michael didn't know. This was one of the most important things I learned in doing this book. Michael knew he did unusual things and he knew he was not understood. He understood himself perfectly. Why couldn't everyone else?

What Michael could not understand was our treatment of him as less than human. Michael by nature was a person who did not look at his friend Dave and see a burned person. He did not look at those dying children and see sickness. He saw the person. He did not look at a person and see black or white. He simply saw the person. Why then did we not do the same with him?

To Michael he was a person who sometimes could not figure things out and an adult who liked childlike things and to be with children. He was an adult and a child. It was everyone else who could not understand. "It's not a mystery. There is no mystery," Michael once said.

Michael didn't know what he was because in order to figure it out he needed to use the part of the brain that he didn't have. Those around him didn't help because they either thought he was an eccentric genius or were just confused.

Mostly though people just believed the lie and they did so because he was so right brain brilliant, in charge of the situation when he was performing, and so wealthy. Had he not been the story would have been totally different.

It is so important to understand this. I didn't understand it completely either at first. More than anything you have to understand that Michael didn't know what was wrong in his life. He had no clue why people behaved as they did toward him. His concept was that the tabloids were being mean and "not nice" and that he made perfect sense. It wasn't that he lied, though he often did for work purposes or protection, as any eight year old or businessman would. It was more the fact that he, himself was trying to make sense of it all. He was told he was a genius, he was told he was brilliant and he believed it. Why wouldn't he? He couldn't dispute that because that would have taken left brain logic. Plus, right brain, he was a genius.

By the end of his life, I think the confusion had gotten worse. As I read things about Michael I realized how many people tried to help him. I thought originally there were none. But there were too many and all of those people were working on the assumption that they were dealing with the normal mentality of an adult or a genius one. They were as confused as he was because he too was working on the same assumption with a disability on top of that.

A head spinning amount of input from well-wishers who really liked and loved him poured into my brain as I read about him just as it must have poured into his. My mind was filled with tons and tons of philosophies and suggestions and input that all were not working and could never work for Michael.

Years of trying to understand with no proper input from someone who would have known how to tell him and what to tell him and years of thinking he was alone in this was taking its toll along with health issues.

I watched so many interviewers, Oprah, Diane Sawyer, Barbara Walters, Rabbi Shmuley Boteach trying to make sense of the situation not only for journalism but for him. People tried so desperately to understand him and to help him, but again they were coming from a point of view of normalcy with no knowledge that the situation that Michael was in even existed. The list is huge of the people who tried to save him from the inevitable, from being the "fawn in the burning forest". I thank them and am happy for their attempts.

Of the animatronic ET Michael said, 'He was so real that I was talking to him." I kissed him before I left. The next day I missed him." (57)

It was this statement that made me understand one reason for the closeness Michael needed to have with children. The loneliness was so deep and deeper than for most because he was so right brain active meaning he really loved everyone, everyone he could not reach.

It will be very hard to understand what he was going through unless you put yourself in that position. Think back to when you were five years old, contemplate it and keep it in mind. What would you be doing all day? You would be playing. Take playing away from a five year old and they cry. Imagine in one instance every person who is five years old like you disappears. They are gone and the only thing left is adults. You are basically the same.

You make some friends eventually but as time goes on even the children you knew and could possibly be close to grew. They left you. Your world is still as a five year old though your body is getting taller. You want to play. You follow the adults and do what you are told as five year olds do.

As time goes on you stay the same but your body changes and what is expected of you becomes more difficult. You are five but your body is in its teens. There are others with teen bodies but you are not one of them. And again there is no one else your age in the world.

When you get to be twenty you grow to be about six and a half or maybe seven and still want to play. You are completely sick of being the only child in the world and you are so very lonely. You make a friend for the first time and you can't wait to see him and hang out with him. You want him with you every moment.

Adults are confused but you understand somewhat. You're just a little boy finally enjoying some friends if only the adults, the "normals" (as Michael called them) would let you. They keep writing things about you and saying things about you and expecting you to know things you don't know.

Now you are eight years old and you want to be normal since you are now thirty also. You want to goof around and see what it would be like to lay in a hyperbaric chamber and still like to play as eight year olds do. You still have not met anyone like you and are begging to find out why you are the only one who is an adult and a child. Still no answer. You are now caught between two worlds and know it. You really want to live in both worlds. And still there is no one you know who is also caught between these two worlds.

"Foreign" that is an important word because it perfectly, just perfectly describes what he was. There was no one like him that he knew of, no one in the world no matter how many people he met and how far he searched. If I could have met Michael, I would have told him, "you are not alone". There are other Peter Pans out there. If he knew just that, he would have been free. I would have told him he is not Peter Pan in his heart. He is Peter Pan in his head. And there are others.

Chapter 17

Sick Man

Today the main headline said, "Michael Jackson was healthy when he died".

What? Huh? What?

How is that possible? Did he get hit by a train and we missed it?

The absolute garbage by the media goes on and on.

Oh, but his lungs were inflamed. Huh? That's healthy?

Now that we know so much and in the words of Michael Jackson, "Oh my God".

Understanding Michael takes understanding that he was physically sick. There is so much crap on the Internet about Michael that I just wanted to stick to what people should know.

Michael's friend and doctor told us in an interview that he had Lupus. I am assuming that we can bank on that testimony. I happen to have a friend with Lupus. I called him to get first hand insight into the disease. Let me tell you about him. He has a business in a two story building but never goes on the second level because it is too painful to use the stairs. He also was terrified of getting sick and terrified of compromising his immune system in any way. Though I hadn't seen him in years he was willing to tell me all I needed to know. As he educated me on this disease and the part stress played in making it worse, I realized the toll the disease had taken on Michael especially when he was under so much stress.

Right brain active and left brain impaired people tend to be very kissy/huggy people. I had seen Michael kiss people often and once saw him grab a fan and give her a kiss. Michael was known for getting too close to fans and those fans could have made him sicker than he was. Maybe that is why he needed to use the mask. Maybe he needed to be protected from himself!

Videos on YouTube, thank God for YouTube, showed Michael's fingers purple and blue and bandages on his fingers. Michael was reported to be on antidepressants when or before he died. Truthfully, with all I have learned about him, his illnesses and the horrible way he was treated in his life, if I were him I'd take antidepressants too. When he said he was in prison he wasn't exaggerating.

I believe Michael had the diseases below because of things told to us in interviews and visible indicators.

Here is a little blurb from a Lupus website that may explain this situation. [58]

Raynaud's Disease: Do your fingers and toes feel numb in the cold? That's a symptom of Raynaud's, which can attack these extremities as well as the nose, lips and ears. It's much more than garden-variety cold hands, though. The skin turns white then blue as blood vessels constrict or spasm. The cause isn't known, but Raynaud's occurs as a secondary condition in patients with various autoimmune diseases. Calcium channel blockers and vasodilators are sometimes prescribed, and other drugs, including Viagra and Prozac, are being studied for Raynaud's.

Attacks the nose? Hmmm. We knew he had this because he started to wear bandages on his fingers. Was it just another crazy Michael Jackson thing? Oh, but if you understood there would be no crazy Michael Jackson things, just crazy reporters and crazy fans and a sick man. Is that the same nose that he had changed because his father told him it was ugly? Hmm is that the same nose that he was so ashamed of?

Prozac. Isn't that an antidepressant? Oh, and Viagra? That was a laugh. Imagine, just imagine, the controversy and gossip and rumors what would have flown around the world if he had tried Viagra to help his always bandaged fingers. It would have gone on for years.

Lupus: As I stated before, I had a friend who has Lupus. He was deathly afraid of getting sick because it could become so serious medical situation for him. When Michael started to wear masks the frenzy started again. Is it for attention? Is it because his nose had fallen off? The garbage went on and on as usual.

The fans, as they had shown us in the past, care for themselves and not for Michael. When they yelled his name over and over into the night in front of his hotel it was obvious. When they yelled, "We want Michael, We want Michael" it was obvious. They would do for them. They would do what they wanted no matter if it kept him from sleeping, no matter if it made him sick.

Michael was surrounded by fans who would do anything they could to get a touch of him or hug him or kiss him or whatever. Would they stop and say, "Hey, maybe I should forgo this opportunity to hug Michael Jackson because I have a cold?" NOT IN YOU'RE LIFE! They would hug him or do whatever they wanted no matter if they had swine flu.

Michael had an immunodeficiency disease and had crowds around him some not twelve inches from him in all directions in layers for yards. Could any of them be sick? Duh! He knew that and he did what he had to do to survive. Good for him. Look at this video to see how bad it could get. [59]

Vitiligo: One or two in a hundred of us develops it, half before the age of 20. Vitiligo causes patches of the skin to lose pigment, and it's theorized than immune dysfunction may be the cause. Corticosteroids may restore pigmentation, and other topical ointments can help. New studies are exploring the use of Ginkgo Biloba and Piperine, a chemical in black pepper, to treat the condition.

Years ago, Michael Jackson told Oprah he has Vitiligo. Ah yes, again. That explains so much including the umbrella. Michael didn't seem to think was so bizarre. Neither does Kim Basinger who carries one everywhere. Maybe we all should take up that odd behavior.

Remember, Michael tried everything to get better. He tried natural health nurses who used teas, gurus, spiritual leaders, religion of all kinds, and medicine of all kinds. You name it he tried it. If you were him, wouldn't you? But if you tried it, it wouldn't be front page news.

Insomnia: Michael must have had insomnia for many years. He stated he could not sleep after a show because he was so wound up. In reference to the death of Diana: "I woke up and a doctor gave me the news and I fell back down in grief and started to cry…" Wait a minute. You woke up with a doctor right there? How long was Michael getting help with sleep? Why would a doctor be there at his side when he woke up? Why would he be needed? I wondered if a sleep test was ever done on Michael.

I always thought the rich had the best doctors because they could afford them. Boy, was I wrong. Some doctors would sure lose a lot of money if a common $10 drug could have put him to sleep. But that's just speculation.

As for drugs plain and simple... he needed them. He didn't want them. He wasn't taking crack cocaine. He needed medicine. Those telling him to stop doing drugs were fighting a futile battle. He could not stop. He was in too much pain. He was sick and had a disease that was extremely painful. He was in extreme pain especially since he was fifty years old and jumping on a stage all night. He was in pain and could not sleep.

One person on the Internet asked why he signed that he could do the shows when he was so sick. I want to answer that. He said he could do ten shows because he needed the money, or so he thought, and because he could do ten shows. He had done it before, I have no doubt. Michael had Lupus for many years. He was told he needed the money for his home and with the pain drugs and sleeping drugs he could have pulled it off. After all it was only ten shows. By the way, who changed it to fifty shows? Where was his lawyer? Gatekeeper?

Oh, and why couldn't he go to the hospital as his nurse friend suggested? Because hospitals use their own doctors and they could have found out things that would either put him in jail or deny him the meds he needed. So, here this multimillion dollar star who has tons of money could not go to a hospital and get the drugs he needed.

Oprah said that Michael's skin was translucent. She stated that you could see the blue veins in his body. I have only seen the effects of vitiligo once when standing on line at the bank and a few times on the television. I thought it odd that Oprah would say Michael's skin was translucent as those other people did not have translucent skin. Then I realized that what I was seeing was through their skin to the fat beneath and Michael being thin and vegetarian did not have fat. Therefore, he would look different than the average person who was of normal size with a normal layer of fat on their body. Also, Raynaud's disease tends to make the body a blue color due to lack of oxygen.

Hyperbaric Chamber: I read today that the hyperbaric chambers were used for various disorders and I know Michael tried everything to get better. The website I went to said that this chamber was helpful for "compromised skin flaps and graphs," plastic surgery (speed healing, reduce scar and infections), slow healing wounds and arthritis. Maybe Michael should have tried it. Oh, that's right; he did and got crucified for it.

Michael needed drugs. He needed them to survive. It was that simple. What is sad is that in our country we dictate what drugs a person can and cannot have no matter whether they need them or not. "Here, Michael Jackson, this is the only drug that will help you sleep but you can't legally have it." Why? These were not drugs for recreation. He was not getting high. He was trying to survive. Who is to say you can't have this medication that you need?

Knowing Michael was so sick answered some more questions like why he would back out of shows and cost himself tons of money in lawsuits. Maybe he was really a sick.

In the news today it stated that Michael had arthritis in his lower spine. In the book by Rabbi Shmuley Boteach, Michael asked his doctor for drugs and the doctor told the rabbi that Michael asked for "a quantity of drugs that could kill a horse." I believe that Michael really needed those drugs. He had been in pain for so long and it was so severe. Michael said, "Shmuley, He's wrong. I have a high tolerance. I'm used to this. I'll be fine." Michael was telling the truth, again. Had Dr. Murray given Michael the drugs he needed he might have been fine. He had been sleeping that way for years or decades.

Michael once said that he lost ten pounds for each show he did. That means at the end of the tour he would have lost fifty pounds. Just an added thought.

What pain it must have been to have lupus and have to jump on stage with those fifty year old joints and arthritis in his spine, with Raynaud's disease and everything else. How much pain he must have been in. I bet it was excruciating.[60]

Now that I know more about Michael, and what I believe to be true of Michael, I realized how honest he really was. He was as honest as he could be and he tried to communicate with us. I realized that whatever he said, I will believe. He was not crazy and didn't do things for attention, meanness, avoidance or to steal from people. The things he did were done because he was eight years old, his logic was a bit off, he was very physically sick, he had too many opinions thrown at him, tabloids loved to lie about him. That is what they were doing. At the same time he supported his family and people all over the world.

The point of this chapter is not to guess at what was ailing Michael. It is not to diagnose and figure out. The point of this chapter is to show that the things he did made sense no matter what the actual ailments were. He was sick and he was sane. He was believable. He was understandable.

Chapter 18

The Bedroom

"There are other times when you like to … be in your pajamas go to sleep. Cut of the light (gestures) Chick ding. Go to sleep. Lay down. That's your private space. You go in the park. I can't go in the park so I create my own park at Neverland… The star needs some space. He has a heart. He's human." Michael Jackson [61]

Michael's room:

Imagine being a little boy, just a normal little boy. You come home from a day at school, walk in the door of your house and say "Hi" to your mother in the kitchen. Then you go to your room and call some friends. The friends come over and hang out in your room or the living room or just play ball outside. While you are hanging out with your friend do you invite your lawyer? Do you invite the maid? Do you invite 150 adults of various jobs and ages to be with you and your friend? No? Why not? It would be ridiculous. What normal boy would do that? What normal boy would want all those people around hanging out with his friend?

Michael Jackson had a house filled with just those people. People were absolutely everywhere. There were cleaning people and stocking people and security guards and butlers and handlers and gatekeepers and businessmen and visitors and grounds keepers and video people, the list goes on and on. Some whose names he may have not even have known. The only place that was his home was his bedroom. That was his only real HOME. So, he invited them, his friends, upstairs to his room-his home. His two story bedroom home.

According to Macaulay Culkin, Michael's bedroom was two stories. It was quite messy as the room of an eight year old or even a teenager would be. It was cluttered with stuff especially, since he had to fit everything that was really his into that room. That would be a place where he could play "The Applehead Club". Remember the "Applehead Club"? Look it up if you don't. (62)

So, to ask Michael, eight year old Michael, to not invite people into his bedroom was like saying you can never have anyone over your house and to top it off, you can never go out to play with them either. You have to stay in this one, although quite large, area for all of your life if you want to play.

Why couldn't he tell us? Why couldn't he just say, "Here's the situation"? He couldn't tell us because "There's a Hole in the Bucket, Dear Liza, there's a hole". He wasn't able to express it. That was the impairment. In addition, he could not for the life of him understand why we didn't understand.

Why couldn't we understand that the bedroom thing was not sexual? Because we were not like him and he was not like us. He might as well been speaking Chinese and we might as well have been speaking Swahili.

There were stairs to climb to get to Michael's room and locks on the doors, which was a point of contention for the prosecutors and others. I wondered if he slept in those wigs and that makeup. What a great financial reward some sleazy, like they are not all sleazy, tabloid reporter would gotten for those pictures.

144

I want to add to this that Michael was wealthy virtually all of his life. They moved when he was around six. Therefore, when we think of a bedroom we are thinking of something that is ten feet by ten feet. With that in mind it is not odd that people would wonder how someone could hang out there for days.

The bedrooms Michael knew were huge bedrooms of the rich. His bed was also huge, not big, huge. Remember his bedroom when he lived with his parents had arcades and such in it. Michael's bedroom was the size of some people's house and on top of that he was an entertainer and on top of that he was eight years old. Therefore, hanging out in Michael's bedroom was like visiting someone in their house. And even if he had seen smaller bedrooms he would not have made the connection that people were thinking of a bedroom that was ten by ten because he would have needed his left brain to do so.

Sleeping in Michael's bed:

I would like to make a point about Michael sleeping in the same bed as children. If Michael was really eight years old his preference would be to hang out with someone of his age as it would be with any eight year old. It would also be someone, preferably his own sex as it would be with any eight year old.

The Jackson children, meaning Michael's brothers slept in bunk beds all in the same room. There were only two bedrooms in the house and the parents had one and the boys another. The girls slept in the living room according to a book by Jermaine's ex-wife. Michael was used to sleeping with bodies in the room. Marlon slept next to him all of his childhood.

Why couldn't they understand? It would have taken left brain logic to explain why what he did as a child and all of his life was not right as he got older. I found many, many things that Michael did as an adult were things that he did as a child or someone who was an adult did that came across to him as right. Many things he was accused of were done by those he considered authority figures who were doing right.

Is it possible that Michael had no idea why he had to have people sleep in his room, why he had to have the lights on and cartoons playing? Absolutely. Michael would not be able to put together the connection between the monster and the children in the bedroom. Even if someone was able to convey to him the connection and make him see they were related and along with that make the situation into a story that became right brain he would have needed left brain to logically reverse those thoughts. Reversing a thought takes left brain ability and a lot of it.

If someone told him that the monster that broke into the room in the middle of the night in a fright mask, wielding a knife to teach the boys not to leave the window open was why he needed children in his room they would still have to work on reversing the thoughts that made him need them there. The story would not have been enough.

There had to have been comfort in the fact that there were other kids in the room. Maybe to hide behind. Maybe to protect. Just their being there would have been a comfort. Just the thought that with all those bodies there, it won't be yours that that knife came down to pierce.

All of this would have had to have been dealt with. It would have had to be moved from logic to story and done so repeatedly until it was understood and the concept grasped. Maybe the fear would have been too much and the concept never accepted. I believe that would have been the case here. The fear was much too great.

Comfort and protection are right brain abilities. The ability to know why it is comforting is left brain. Therefore, he knew he needed that comfort but he couldn't explain why and didn't know himself why. And to him it's nothing. What's the big deal?

The mother of the first accuser: On their third visit to Neverland, she said she refused her son's request to spend the night with Jackson in his bedroom. But she relented during a trip to Las Vegas in March 1993, after Jackson—whom she described as "sobbing, crying, shaking and trembling" –confronted her, she testified. "You don't trust me. We're a family," she quoted the entertainer as saying. "There's nothing wrong. There's nothing going on. Why don't you trust me?' After 30 to 40 minutes of pleading by Jackson, the mother said she relented, and the two then began sleeping in the same bed on nights when they were together.

The nurse on the television after his death said he slept with the lights on and cartoons on the computer. But when the others slept in his bed including adults it seemed he was able to sleep. I hadn't read anywhere where he had to leave the lights on when others slept in his room or that he couldn't sleep. In all I read he slept fine when there was another person in the room. He probably slept best with someone who was not "foreign" to him meaning an adult, a "normal".

So, sleeping with children in the same bed was not sexual nor was it sweet. It was something he needed. He needed it to really sleep. It was friendly, non-lonely and safe.

I would like to add to this that it was the nighttime when such severe loneliness would have been most felt. In the quiet of the night all alone the fact that Michael was totally alone in the world would have hit him the hardest. I believe that someone in his bed with him helped him get through the terrible realization that he was the only person in the world and that he chose the children because they were the closest thing to what he was and he believed the closest to God.

Chapter 19

Sex

I have to say that I was not sure I wanted to write this chapter. I was hoping I could just leave it out but I knew it had to be done. Michael had been beaten up for so long and I didn't want to add to hurting Michael, the child, even if he was in the wrong.

I knew that Michael had a desperate need to be close to children. I knew he had a problem with judgment. I also knew that he had the body of a grown man. That was the part that scared me.

I am a person who would never steal from another and certainly would not put an innocent person in jail so that I could make some money. Therefore, I had a hard time believing there was not wrongdoing on Michael's part. I was biased against Michael in this instance.

I have to admit that I honestly thought him guilty not of molesting children but of going beyond the desperate closeness into the sexual realm. Michael denied it repeatedly which is the action he probably would have taken guilty or not, so I didn't put much credence in that.

The "Normal" drive us crazy:

I would like to tell you a story that shows what happens when "normal" people enter the world of those with left brain impairment or in other words the world I worked in. I want to tell you how a situation like this could play out with a left brain impaired person who is living in a normal world. Add to this the fact that Michael didn't have any knowledge that he was impaired. He just knew the rest of the world was different and he was condemned for it.

I can tell you that I had often seen times when the unusual behavior of impaired people would put them in horrible situations including being arrested or placed in mental institutions. I have had to go to mental institutions to get my student out. And this was a high functioning child. It was horribly frightening. I also had one arrested for suspected possession of PCP. In the world of the police she looked like she was on PCP. That is how they would see her.

In my classrooms we had to deal with the situations of sex or better stated sexual body functions often. There were many times I had to call a Dad and tell him that he needed to take his son aside and tell him what to do and where to do it. We would often send boys to the bathroom and tell them to "fix" things. We would often tell parents of girls to tell the girls that they are to go in their room and take care of what needs to be tended to. I worked mainly with teenagers and adults so this was very, very common. It was not unusual, it was not embarrassing, it was not abnormal. It was just part of every day teaching.

That everyday teaching was part of OUR world. If I had told a boy in the regular classes to go to the bathroom and take care of things I might have ended up in the news. Our world is the one Michael belonged in; the other world is the one he lived in. That was why he was so confused and lonely.

I am going to tell you a story showing the difference between the world of damaged children and the world of normal adults. The difference is huge. The misunderstanding is huge. This story involves students with severe left and right brain impairments. The one who instigated the situation was so severely handicapped that he did not belong in a regular school nor was he able to read. Of course, they were not like Michael but the purpose of this story is to show how things with special children mixing with the regular population can...go...crazy.

We had an instance when two boys doing what they should not have done where they should not have been was seen by people who were not like us. All...hell...broke...loose. Parents were called in. Lawyers were called in. More lawyers were called in. The Superintendant was called in. PR people were called in. We were isolated so we couldn't talk to anyone. What was told to one parent scared the life out of her because it was conveyed in a completely wrong way by a person who should have never been an administrator in the first place.

As for me, I was forbidden to talk to any parent because the lawyers were involved. The parents were looking to me for answers, which was the norm for us. IT WAS A MESS. The parents, when they found out what really happened, said, "What the heck?" The kids were saying, "What the heck?" Every person in our world was saying, "What the heck?" Every normal person was saying, "The sky is falling, the sky is falling."

The whole thing was "much ado about nothing". It was a mole hill blown up into Mount Vesuvius because the leaders involved were normal thinking people who had no clue what they were doing or what they were dealing with. Had all involved been normal it would have been a different story but they were not.

Had I seen the boys rather than a normal person I would have sent them back to the room, called their parents and had a talk of what happened. I also would have been very mad at the boys not for what they did but for not going directly from point A to point B as they were supposed to.

Much ado about nothing, absolutely nothing, was the story of these two kids and could have been the story of Michael if anything actually did take place. Remember, a lot of money was involved and honestly, I have gotten a new respect for the concept that people would sell family and their souls for money from doing this book. I saw it often in this research.

Michael was desperate for someone to be close to him and he felt closest to those who were what he was as an injured person, which is an eight year old boy. To young boys, girls are not an interest because they are psychologically building who they are. Guys hang with guys. Michael fought this battle all of his life. His situation was not a grown man hanging out with young children. It was a situation of a guy hanging out with his peers.

Sex and girlfriend/boyfriend relationships are built each day as the child interacts with other children. That growing is left brained as well as right brained. Michael did not learn about these relationships because of his disability, because he worked most of the time he should have been learning and socially growing and because the correct input was not being given to him. That input would have been given to him through other special children and specialized teaching. So, it was a double whammy.

Sex and the left brain impaired:

If anything was done with the children it would have been not for sexual gratification. It could have been for physical gratification but I don't think so. I will tell you why. Physical gratification could have been obtained any time. There was something much more important to Michael. What was infinitely more important to Michael would have been to have close friends to play with and what he cried about all his life which was getting to be the adult through being the little boy.

If anything happened with the children, if anything was done to cross over the line, it would have been for one of three reasons.

The first reason would have been to impress the child so the child would like him and hang out with him like the frumpy teenager who follows the pretty popular teenager around doing anything to impress the popular teen.

It is a "natural state of being" for eight year old boys to hang out with eight year old boys but they don't have to do without it for twenty years and then try to catch up. Michael was deprived of the normal growing with peers. He was taking a natural path toward growing but was so starved for it that was possible he might have taken things too far. Not only was he anxious and desperate to go down the path to get to the place where the grown boy would be but he was so grateful to those children who would help him get there. That gratitude was what made him kiss Emmanuel Lewis on the cheek and call him his "best friend". All of this was without conscious knowledge of what was happening and why and with impaired judgment.

The second reason would be to just be joking around with left brain impairment. I had seen it many times with students I had worked with. Michael liked to tickle his friends. That was seen by others according to some books I had read. No big deal. Michael was a joker. No big deal. But with a left brain impairment would a child, which Michael was, tickle in private places just for a joke or just not particularly watching what he was doing? Yes, it is possible.

Doing this would depend on what he was taught and how he was taught. How he was taught is very important because being taught improperly can cause a whole list of problems. I am assuming that Michael was not taught by special education professionals.

This situation would have had an especially hard impact on the children that Michael was with because he would be joking with the child and not know he was doing something improper or really improper and hurting the child. He would tickle or touch the boy as a joke then go on being Michael and joking in other ways and the boy would be shocked that he was one minute a friend joking then touching him inappropriately then being a friend joking again. It would make him seem a friend who could suddenly turn cold and callous and then turn back to a friend. It would leave the child in a state of complete confusion and wondering whether others would do the same.

The third reason is to teach with left brain impairment. If there was anything that happened with the child in the last case it might have been to teach. Michael always felt responsible to fix the whole world. The child said that Michael asked him sexual questions and warned him of the things that could happen if he didn't take care of things properly. I am sure what he was telling the boy was for the child's own good if the conversation really took place. As I said before, teaching sex improperly to a left brain impaired person can lead to a whole list of problems.

A person teaching a left brain impaired person about sex would tell him and maybe show him this is what you do and it's okay to do this because it is normal. It is a normal part of growing and you need to take care of things properly or bad things could happen. Therefore, the left brain impaired person would not be inhibited in telling another child nor would he think it was "sexual". Just as the person teaching Michael was not being sexual neither would Michael if he taught another person.

Think of the confusion here. A normal adult tells Michael that this and this is okay and normal and something you have to take care of and then normal adults tell him it is wrong and take him to court for doing what someone told him was ok. Maybe that person even assisted him at the time. Who knows? There were so many people in Michael's life it had my head spinning.

As I said previously, I believed that Michael was guilty not of molesting children but in desperate loneliness with left brain impairment went too far to be close to those he thought to be the only people in the world.

If Michael did anything with these boys what happened is a mole hill that became Mount Vesuvius but...

Then...in my research I discovered things that made me wonder if my belief was partially if not completely wrong.

Chapter 20

The Accusations

In the interview with Diane Sawyer she asked Michael if he had touched the boys or fondled them or whatever sexually. He said, "No, No, No". Then you can hear him say in a quiet revealing tone, "I'm not interested in that." I could picture the Handlers and Gatekeepers jumping out of their shoes at his admission that he was not interested in sex.

There were four things that bothered me when relating to the first molestation charges.

First was Michael's quiet statement that he was not interested in "that". This statement would be very common among my students and they honestly are not interested in "that". In fact, it is extremely rare for these students to be interested in sex.

The second thing was the boy's control over Michael. This child who was thirteen years old had an unusual understanding of Michael or I should say of people like Michael just as I do. I believe that to Michael he was someone who would not leave because he would always understand him even as he grew. Therefore being the only person ever who would be in his life always and never become a "normal".

In the Tamborelli book he tells the story of when Michael and the boy were friends and that whenever the boy got up from the table Michael would follow him to the point that the boy finally said, "Michael, I'm going to the bathroom."

This boy had control over Michael not the other way around.

The third thing was that the child didn't complain about Michael to anyone.

The fourth thing was "truth serum". At the end of this chapter you will see information about truth serum and the statement that the person given such serum "tends to regurgitate a cocktail of information which is a blend of facts and fantasy".

Here is what easily may have happened. Maybe it was in addition to Michael going a bit too far with a friend or maybe with him being completely innocent.

With this scenario there is no one guilty and no one lying; not Michael, not the child and not the father. It was just a mistake which seems to be par for the course in the story of Michael Jackson.

Michael met a boy who for the first time understood him not as a child or an icon but as a person who had a handicap. He so much wanted and needed this person to be in his life because this is a person who could stay for real and forever. So he did all he could to be near him and would not let him out of his sight except to go to the bathroom as stated above.

Michael wrote things to the boy asking him never to be "conditioned" which was the term Michael used for what changed the children into the adults that he believe let down the world. He also told the boy he wanted him to stay with him forever at Neverland.

To the boy's father Michael was a famous, powerful and rich celebrity who was controlling his son. Sleeping at Michael's gave the father the impression that Michael was using his son or preparing his son for a sexual relationship with him.

The boy denied that anything inappropriate was happening and the boy's mother tried to tell the father that Michael was just a big kid himself. As time went on Michael became more desperate to see what he perceived as the only person in the world and be closer to him. This convinced the father, despite denial from the boy and mother, that Michael was doing things with the boy that he should not do.

The father wanting to help his son and being a dentist had access to drugs He decided to give the child "truth serum" to find out what was really going on. Now here is where you would have to ask yourself how that would be done. When he injected the child what did he do? Did he simply say what is going on with you and Michael or did he provide a list of questions with sexual acts and ask if those acts were acted upon?

According to my reading, truth serums are no longer used because of the fact that what takes place when the person is under can become suggestive and be something the person actually believes to be true.

This was shocking to me as I had always thought this drug or these types of drugs were real and foolproof. I guess I watched too much Hollywood on that one. Apparently, so did the father.

So the boy who would not say anything was happening with Michael suddenly was saying that things happened. The mother then had to side with the boy believing as I did that truth serum is foolproof.

The boy now believing that Michael is guilty is told that he is obligated to do something to prevent Michael from doing harm to other boys so he and his father file charges.

According to people near Michael he didn't want to pay any money to make the accusations go away. He wanted to go to court. My first thought was that Michael was sick with an illness that got worse with stress so he paid them to keep from making his illness worse.

That thought lasted only a brief second. Though I do believe that was a small part of the reason for payment the real reason, since there was no real physical evidence that was undisputable, had to do with the Gatekeepers.

I believe that a battle raged continuously for years concerning Michael and it started long before this boy was in the picture. The battle by the Gatekeepers was to keep the "secret" that Michael was handicapped from the public.

I believe too that those who were not in the loop who were around Michael believed that his being with children was not innocent since they did not know he was handicapped.

As it stood, Michael's paying off the child and his family, made him look like a child molester to many people. But he was still the icon and the secret that he was actually handicapped was still a secret.

Another thing that surprised me was the statement in the Tamborelli book that Michael was always "blindsided" when trouble hit. If he was referring to money troubles and lawsuits that would make sense since Michael had very little to do with who was paid and not paid and what was going on with money. If he was talking about accusations against him he would not have been blindsided if he was guilty.

After the decision to pay the Chandler family Michael finished his last show he left the hotel. After he checked out, the hotel staff was stunned to discover that the carpets in the living room and in Michael's bedroom were stained with vomit. There were deep dents and cracks in the plaster of the living-room wall, as if someone banged his head, or his fists, against it...There were scribblings on the walls ("I love you, I love you") and even on the fabric of some of the furniture." [64]

In the second accusation Michael was told what was happening and his reply was, 'huh?"

That doesn't sound like the statement of a guilty person to me.

The story with the second accuser was so beyond ridiculous. If the first accuser was not there no attorney would have taken this to court considering this family had a history of doing this same thing to JC Penney years before.

The following excerpt is from Wikipedia:

In August 1998 the Arvizo family was detained on a shoplifting charge at a J.C. Penney department store in West Covina, California. According to J.C. Penney, Gavin and Star Arvizo were sent out of the store by their father with an armload of stolen clothes, the family was detained and Janet started a "scuffle" with security officers. The shoplifting charge was dropped, but Janet filed a lawsuit for US $152,000, saying that when she was detained she was "viciously beaten" by three security officers, one of whom was female. The psychiatrist hired by J. C. Penney to evaluate Janet Arvizo found her to have rehearsed her children into supporting her story and to be both "delusional" and "depressed," although Janet's own doctor found her to be only the latter. More than two years after the original alleged incident Janet added a further charge that one of the male officers had "sexually fondled" her breasts and pelvis area for "up to seven minutes". Ultimately the department store settled out of court with the family for US $75,000.

There were supposedly five others who were molested by Michael. Comically one was McCauley Culkin who was at Michael's funeral and repeatedly said nothing happened. One other is a person my family knows who states to this day nothing happened. The others I didn't even bother to research.

I know that Michael was not capable of the act of molestation. I know there were very strange circumstances in the accusers. I know that hundreds of children slept in the bed with Michael and other children and though the attorneys searched the world for others to come forward none did.

Truth serum information:

All of these truth serums work in the same manner: They depress the central nervous system and interfere with judgment and higher cognitive function. A person in such a state tends to regurgitate a cocktail of information which is a blend of facts and fantasy, with many details exaggerated or omitted. In a word, unreliable.

In 1963 the Supreme Court ruled that a confession produced under the influence of truth serum was unconstitutionally coerced, and therefore inadmissible. After that, the use of such drugs fell rapidly from popularity in the U.S..

But are these truth serums effective? Do they produce any useful results?

The short answer is, no. The long answer is "Noooooooooooo!" while running in slow-motion.

Many barbiturates fall under the "truth serum" category, including scopolamine, sodium amytal, and Sodium Pentothal. Scopolamine was tested in the 1950s as a truth serum in project MKULTRA, and is now infamous as a date-rape drug due to its tendency to cause retrograde amnesia (the inability to recall events prior to its administration). Sodium Pentothal is a drug which is commonly used in operating rooms as general anesthesia, though in recent years it has been largely replaced by better alternatives.
http://www.damninteresting.com/the-truth-about-truth-serum

Wikipedia: In reality there is no such thing as a real truth serum as most people would imagine. Things that are considered truth serums are drugs that lower a person's inhibitions which should in theory cause the person to tell more truth. The problem is that many drugs used as a TS are CNS depressants such as ethyl alcohol, barbiturates, and other similar sedatives. The problem with sedative is they lower cognitive function and memory, this often leads to a subject mixing fantasy with fact.

Another thing that adds to the unreliability of TS drugs are that they often simply increase talking but not actual truth telling.

"Togetherness...that's all I'm after"

I am going to tell you not what I believe but what I know. Michael did not...molest...anyone. All he wanted was to have a real friend but didn't know how.

Macaulay once said of Michael, "We are going to be eight years old forever. Of course, like all the others, Macaulay grew up.

"I have all of this...yet I have nothing. The things I really want in my life are the things I don't have. The only thing that matters in life is having someone who understands you, who trusts you and will be with you when you grow old, no matter what." Michael Jackson sitting in a tree at Neverland

Michael walked the earth completely alone. No one understood his handicap nor did they understand his brilliance.

"Togetherness...that's all I'm after."

So true, so true.

Chapter 21

Trial and Terror

His hands were shaking, his heart pounding, his face called gaunt by the media was whiter than usual. He looked numb. He stood there so unlike Michael. Slow moving and obviously in shock. I can see it now. It broke my heart. Terror is the word that described that day for Michael Terror, terror, terror, terror and death for the eight year old boy with a heart of gold.

"He tries, God knows he does, and it's hard for him. I saw it first-hand. He is sick before going on camera for an interview, throwing up, so nervous, so upset, so filled with anxiety. Your heart goes out to him. You wonder how he ever ended up in the public eye, and what an ordeal he has been through just to get this far in it. [63]

The truth is that if Michael was convicted he would probably have been better off dying. Watch a prison movie and look at those men in that prison and think of what that would have been like for the sweet soul little boy.

One juror said, "I can't believe this man could sleep in the same bedroom for 365 days and not do something more than watch television and eat popcorn."

Let's change the quote. "I can't believe this boy could sleep in the same bedroom (that is the size of a small house) for 365 days and not do something more than watch television and eat popcorn," Believable it now?

Oh and, 365 days? Michael worked like a dog. He would not be home anywhere near 365 days.

To show how much he worked I only have this statistic. In 1987 Michael performed over 123 concerts in a year and a half in fifteen countries on four continents. That was his typical pace. No way was he home 365 days of the year.

Bashir: Do you think it would be true to say that you've found friendship and inspiration in children that you haven't been able to find in adults?

Michael: "That's absolutely the truth."

Bashir: Really?

Michael: "Yes, yes, I haven't been betrayed or deceived by children. Adults have let me down. Adults have let the world down". (65)

Jury Foreman Rodriguez: "We felt that Michael was still a kid in a man's body"

Grown men don't hang out with chimpanzees. Grown men don't hang out with little boys. Grown men don't call young children their "best friend".

There are only two possibilities. One is that Michael, eight year old Michael, did things with those children for the reasons already stated or eight year old Michael didn't do anything but "watch television and eat popcorn" and people drew their own wrong conclusions thinking he was a grown man. Or they simply wanted money.

Either way, eight year old Michael would not be guilty. Since the precept if this book is that Michael is eight years old due to disability, as an eight year old he would not be guilty. But maybe he wasn't guilty of anything at all. If perception is so powerful, damage would come from being attracted to wanting to be around children even if nothing happened. I don't know but let's look at the situation.

The following excerpt is Michael's story; or what I believe Michael's story to be.

It's 1993. "I couldn't believe it when they told me. I was being charged with molesting a friend of mine. I looked up molest and this is what it said molest meant: to annoy, disturb, or persecute especially with hostile intent or injurious effect. It also meant: to make annoying sexual advances to; especially: to force physical and usually sexual contact on.

What were they saying I did? They said I forced a child to do things to injure him. "I would slit my wrists before I would hurt a child." Still that is what they said I did. I would not hurt my friend and he was thirteen years old. How could I force him to do things?

Plus he was my friend. We had a pact. He understood me and he was a child. Children are beautiful. Children are pure. Children are close to God. How could a child, this child, do this to me? I don't understand.

They told me I could go to jail and eventually I just told them to make it go away. I was already sick and was not supposed to be stressed. I had Lupus and I have breakouts when I am stressed. I also throw up and my fingers get cold and go numb. Sometimes I have to shake my hands to bring the blood to my fingers. Plus this was embarrassing and I am very shy.

I told Diane Sawyer that they said they couldn't guarantee that I would not go to jail so I said, "okay, pay it". I could go to jail for years and years. I was happy in that interview because it was over and I could tell everyone that I was free and that meant they would know that I did not try to molest a child.

It's 2003: I couldn't believe it again when they told me my friend, someone I helped when he was so sick, someone who probably would have died if I didn't invite him to heal at Neverland was charging me with molesting him and kidnapping him. I am the one who told him about Pac Man and to picture Pac Man going through his body eating the cancer. I fed him good food. I paid for him to have the right medications. They said he would die and there he was years later about to take my life from me, about to take a father from his children.

I knew everyone thought it was weird that I liked having kids around. I didn't think anything of it. I needed them. That's all.

I sat there watching this boy, my friend, and his mother telling everyone that I kidnapped him and kept him locked up at Neverland. It really hurt. It made me sick. I don't kidnap people, I don't lock them at my house and I don't injure them and force them. But there they were saying so and I could go to jail.

All I wanted to do was get close to the world. All I wanted to do was show the world who I really was and show them my family. After that documentary that took everything I said and twisted it I was panicked. I could lose my family, my everything. I am going to throw up.

I needed my friend that I helped so much to tell the world that I was not what the documentary portrayed. I needed him to tell the truth. I needed him to say we were friends who cared about each other. I was surely scared. The people around me were just as scared.

I thought Mr. Bashir was a good man. I thought that he was because he did an interview with Princess Diana. Anyone who worked with such a beautiful person as Princess Diana had to be a good man. Why did he do this to me? I guess he was just another adult. Adults let down the whole world so why not me?

I sat there day after day hearing this family that I tried to help saying horrible things about me. I sat there having every thing I had ever done torn apart.

I don't get it. He was saying that I told him about sex stuff so he would know and not do crazy things. It's true that I had seen people do crazy stuff. Even when I was six years old people were doing crazy stuff. The world is crazy but why would it be a bad thing to tell someone something about sex that would keep him safe? People told me sex stuff to keep me safe. My father was the one who was supposed to tell me but forget that. That kid had no father to tell him either. People talked to me about how to take care of my body and stuff. He was thirteen and there was stuff he should know. Why would it be okay for them to tell me and not okay for me to tell him? It's all so confusing.

I gave him a watch and they said it was so I could molest him. I give people things all the time. Now it's wrong. I know now that I will never understand.

The days dragged on and on. Every day I sat there wishing it was over and dreading the day that will come when they may say I will be put in prison.

I just could not get up and face another day. Couldn't they do something to help me? It was too hard. My body was sick and I was hurting. At least I had my doctor to help me sleep. What if I go to jail? Then I'll never sleep again.

I couldn't get dressed this morning. I didn't want to and I couldn't. I was so tired and so sick. I was so scared. I told them I would not go and I fought not to. It was all too hard. I was just so scared. My mother and the others tried to get me to go but I just wanted to hide. Then one of my attorneys came in and said that if I was not there in an hour I will be doing the trial from jail. I thought, "They can make me go but they can't make me get dressed." I told them I would go but I would not change my pajamas. They dragged me in like that. I was sick, I was numb.

Jail meant not seeing my children. Jail meant being surrounded by people who were worse than Joseph. Jail meant no pain medication. Jail meant no sleep medication. Jail meant staying alone completely isolated. Someone once asked me what I would do if there were no children in the world. I said, "It would be over. I would just die." Now here I was maybe being where there are only Joe Jacksons and no children. I would rather die.

My attorney kept telling them or hinting to them or whatever that I was a ten year old boy. I had been telling them that for years. Finally they would understand. Wait, what would that mean to my children? What ungodly thing could they throw at me with that information? What do I tell my children?

My lawyer told them about the mother suing JC Penney for sexual assault on her and getting thousands of dollars. Why do I let people like this in my house? But how do you know who is a good person? Do I stay away from everone? Maybe that would be a good idea. That was funny. Then they would call me a recluse.

This was the last day before the verdict. This could be the last day I would be with my children. This could be the last day I would be home. This could be the last day of everything. I threw up all night. I love them. I don't understand.

I told them I loved them and that things would be alright. I wasn't sure about that last part.

How did Michael survive each day of the three month ordeal that picked him apart bit by bit where his previous belief of children being pure was dashed before his eyes by a child he took care of, a child he called his friend? How could he survive it if he did do something that was done by a logically impaired eight year old boy?

According to one juror, "We felt Michael was a ten year old boy in a man's body." Proof of that must have been presented continuously with each action of Michael's being picked apart and explained. This action, that action picked apart and analyzed right before his eyes labeling him a child, which would have been fine if he was told that there was a reason that he was a child and what it was. But he was told nothing. How did he survive hearing each day the proof that he was a child in a man's body when all of his life he was told he was a genius?

Uri Geller told Michael, "I know you are innocent but you have to understand why there are others who do not believe that. You have to stop with the children in people's faces. You have to try to understand the public. It's not just you. You are in the world." He becomes sad and his eyes glass over.[65]

He couldn't because as he said before, "If there were no children on this earth, if somebody announced all the kids are dead, I would jump off the balcony immediately. I'm done. I'm done."

How did he survive each day knowing that he had an eight year old at home that was probably older than him?

How did he survive each day knowing the children would one day find out how old he really was and wondering what they would think?

How did he survive knowing he had no home to go to since Neverland was raided so brutally and kids can't be there anyway?

How did he survive each day knowing that he may have to spend the rest of his life eating lunch with no hair, no makeup and no protection with murders and rapists?

How did he survive each day with a disease that got worse with stress?

So the truth is... he didn't.

Home:

If that was the first time he heard it, since everyone thought he was such a genius, no wonder he left court not celebrating. What would he tell his kids? That would be enough to make me take antidepressants for sure.

Let's see, you can't have friends your own age, have a family whose motives you often questioned, no hair, no home, no reputation, no dignity, no protection and you're only eight years old. People take alcohol and depression medication to deal with much, much less than that.

Michael wanted friends. If he had limited logical capacity, if he thought he should share with the world not only what he knew about being safe but his money as well what was so wrong? He didn't buy a child a watch to entice him. He gave it to him because he needed friends and didn't go through the normal channels to get them.

I believe the fire was caused by an eight year old boy doing what eight year old boys or thirteen year old boys or whatever age boys do and that it all got out of hand as stories often do. Assuming, anything happened at all.

If you are a kid and so is he what is the big deal? If you were a man trying to seduce a boy to have sex that was another story. That would not have been the story here.

If only they would have let him meet other Peter Pans none of this would have happened. I believe that with all my heart. I believe that loneliness would have been gone, the understanding of why he was "foreign" would be gone and he would not cry any more.

There are other Peter Pans in the world and Michael was searching for them and for himself. I blame those who knowingly kept him from the one thing he needed to survive, the one thing he begged and searched for his whole life, the one thing that caused him to have to be close to children.

Headline:

"An eight year old disabled boy was on trial and today will find out if he will spend what will probably be the rest of his life in prison. This shy disabled boy who has serious diseases including Lupus and severe insomnia will possibly be in prison with child molesters and rapists. This child will probably die from pain, abuse or lack of sleep in prison.

Michael Jackson walked into the court for the last time. This day they would decide his fate. It could have been the last time he would see the outside of a prison. It could have been the last days he would hug his children. It would have been in essence his death sentence, a torturous death. As he walked in with his hands trembling he must have been numb with fear. The proper word would be terror, terror for an eight year old boy. Think of how he would be treated in a prison. Prison! Prison! Think about that. Prison with the most hardened of men. The little boy would be in prison with murderers and rapists. The "sweetest guy I ever knew", the man who wiped the dirt off the dancer and searched for a liver for a sick child now would live in the midst of hard core criminals. For an eight year old boy, think of the terror that he had to go through.

No one except those involved can reveal the motives in the trials. Money could surely be a factor, so can mistake, or both.

As eight year old Michael Jackson walked to what might have been his virtual death there was a camera in his face and an idiot yelling in the background, "Michael". Here he was walking to his possible death with the cage still surrounding him.

Michael might have won his freedom from prison to step outside to the flashing cameras and yelling people. Michael walked out of the courtroom only to walk back into the cage.

Chapter 22

Thank God for the Children, Thank God for Debbie Rowe

Upon Prince being born Michael said, "I have been blessed beyond comprehension. I will work tirelessly being the best father I can be."

The purpose of this chapter is to try to explain what Michael's children really meant to him in regard to the situation he was in and those involved were in. Everything that happened made perfect sense to me and I am hoping I have conveyed it to you so that it makes perfect sense to you too.

The more I researched this situation from the point of view that I have expressed to you the sadder I became for Michael. I needed to know that all was not sad. I wanted to know what really made him happy. Did he really like to perform? He said he did and until he was too old to enjoy it I believe he really did. I know from his own words he hated to go on tour. I know he laughed a lot in his life at most everything. That was good. There had to be some happiness.

I learned a lot from listening to the stories of the people and not the media. I decided to and did believe Debbie and I decided to take the

.

stance that she didn't do what she did for money, which was the only real accusation in question.

Enter Debbie Rowe.

When I first heard about Debbie Rowe I had no opinion. I didn't care much one way or the other. I had enough to do taking care of my own life, my children and the lives of the unusual children that were put in my life who needed my expertise and care.

Today I thank God for her. Today I can understand how someone could love Michael as a friend enough to go through so much. "I think it was seventeen or eighteen years that I knew him when I had Prince. He was such a fabulous man and such a good friend and has always been there for me from the day I met him," Debbie told an interviewer. (40)

"Michael was a fabulous man". I believe Debbie when she says she really did love Michael. First of all, Michael was easy to love. He was kind and cute and loving to many people. If she met him when he was still considered a black man she would have been by his side as he changed color. She would have emotionally walked through the most trying times with him comforting him along the way as a nurse and human being who understood. When you walk with someone who is going through such difficulty you bond with them. Michael was easy to bond with. Michael was easy to love.

Debbie was a caretaker. Debbie was a nurse. She wasn't a business person. She was in the caretaking business from the start. It's easy to get caught in a relationship with someone who is so damaged and so hurt and so sweet and so funny and so loving. She, as a caretaker, went from being a nurse to being a nurse for animals at her home. She is a caretaker by nature.

There are three scenarios with Debbie. One was that she did what she did for Michael because she cared for him. The second was that she

176

did what she did for money. The third was that she sold her kids for money.

Let's say first that she did what she did and had the kids "for him". I truly believe she did care enough for him to have done so for him.

Those who would argue that she did it for money would have to ask themselves what she got for that pain and agony? Did she buy jewelry and fast cars and fly all over the world? Did she hobnob with the rich and famous? No, she stayed alone then bought a horse ranch. If she was a gold digger she was a really bad one.

The tabloids were offering half a million dollars for just a picture of her pregnant. A picture of the kids would have sold for millions and dope on Michael from her would also have sold for millions and continued to do so for a long time. She could have sold so many stories to the tabloids and made a fortune. She could have sold the kids pictures and made a fortune. She never did. If she was in it for money she sure didn't do it right.

Now, after his death, she could, if she wanted to, take the kids with no one having a say because she is really their mother, put them in a house with nannies and housekeepers, put on a show for a while and lived her own life anyway. Then she could have made tons of money. She didn't. So when I hear that she sold the children, I have to say that if money was the motive, again she did a bad job of making it.

The truth is that without money she would have left herself very vulnerable. She would have had no protection from all that could hit her. So, it really needed to be that she received money in the end.

One constant in everything I saw and read was Michael's happiness when he spoke of the children. They made him happy. They made him feel at home. I believe the joy they brought him sustained him through so much. They were his everything.

I remember Michael saying that he was so happy when Prince was born. I remember the look on his face as he spoke of the day. In fact, I would venture to say that it was his extreme happiness to have Prince that made him do what he did when Paris was born. "I took her and ran home with her placenta and all". Can you imagine an adult doing that? No. But can you imagine an eight year old doing such a thing especially if that eight year old was so lonely without the children and happy with them?

The threat always loomed over Michael's head that there was a mother out there who could, suddenly change her mind and want the kids back. This is a horror that many parents of adopted children feel often for their entire lives. Will the biological parent come by and say, "I want my kids back"? He had to be sure that couldn't happen. Blanket was born to parents only he knew or maybe didn't know. But that secured his stability with Michael.

Enter Blanket.

This was another person who would give Michael real love and at his level. That's the key. The key is that they were at his level. I am tempted to say sadly the children grow up but that is not completely the case. Yes, they would grow and part from him in a way in which he needed them to be close but the bond of love, the bond of child and father no matter what would always be there. Knowledge of that made me happy for him. Still, he needed someone who would need him again as an adult and relate to him as a child.

He said that he was so happy being a father and I am so glad for that because it makes knowing what I know so much easier. The children made him human other than Michael Jackson the icon. And as we have seen from them not only did he do a fantastic job of raising them or hiring the right people to help him do so but he loved them with all of his heart and they loved him right back.

Thank God for him that Debbie was there, for whatever her reason. And the reason is really irrelevant anyway. Thank God she was there to give him the family he so desperately needed, the family who would love him always and without condition. Thank God she was there to make him realize that having a family was possible.

Again, what would you do?

If what I read is correct, Debbie stepped back into the children's lives twice. I believe each time she did was because she felt the children were possibly not safe. I believe her to be a good person who really just wanted to give her friend a wonderful gift that he in fact really needed and that she really did love him. She said she called him to see what was going and he didn't return her calls.

I think that he didn't know how to tell what was going on. I know that often when he would be challenged he would fire someone or avoid situations not because he was hiding but because he really could not make sense of things and didn't know what to say or do.

Debbie said two things. She said that she is "stepping up" and that "We had an agreement... he didn't keep his end," What could that agreement have been? Money? Perhaps. Or maybe it was that the kids will always be with him in his care and especially not near Joe Jackson. I am sure she heard many teary stories over those seventeen years.

I have read some nasty things about Debbie Rowe but let's assume that what came from her friend is true. If the deal was that Michael was to take care of the kids and now suddenly Joe Jackson will be in their lives I would be scared too. Leaving Katherine the kids invited Joe in and we know right from the start that he thought he was boss. We heard it from him in numerous ways. We saw it. I know it would have scared me if I were her.

Michael needed those children. Michael got a glimpse of what it would be like to really be human and fit into someone's world not as a caretaker to a needy person or the financial caretaker, which he had been to so many but to really, really fit. With the birth of Paris he had it all, one girl and one boy. But that could not be enough. He needed a big family. When Debbie could not have any more children she said she was of no use to him anymore. I believe that to be true but not in a selfish way. They were friends and Michael didn't just want children. He needed them. Knowing what I know and the situation he was in made me realize that the children were not just children but the air he needed to breathe. It wasn't that Debbie meant nothing but that he was suffocating and he needed that air. The air the children provided.

I would like to add, many parents give their children to others if they feel it is better for the child. Those who cannot properly take care of the child, for whatever reason, take this action out of love for the child. It's called adoption. It is not questioned by anyone. The children are happy, the parents are happy. Everyone is fine.

Debbie had known Michael for seventeen years. She saw him go through the horrendous situation of losing the color of his skin. They formed a bond and she loved him as she had stated. She knew that Michael for years before Prince was born took care of child after child. He cared for burn victims, children who were cancer patients, children with diseases of all kinds. Why wouldn't she think she was putting the children in good hands? He was already a loving father figure to so many. Those who knew Michael loved him. They stated it so numerous times. So, why is this situation so hard to understand? It makes perfect sense to me.

I know there are no words to express what those children meant to someone like Michael. To say they were his life would be the understatement of the century. Thank God for those children.

I think if there wasn't so much controversy and there weren't so many financial problems Michael would have had children every few years and been very happy in his life with that. In fact he stated that he wanted to adopt a child from each continent.

In addition I would like to say the kids' father is Michael Jackson. Adopted children don't have to go through this. Michael Jackson is their father. He is the one who loves them and loved them to the end. He was their father.

END OF STORY.

As an added note, caring for children is very right brained. Disciplining them is very left brained and Michael left the discipline to Grace just as he left the hard confronting business things to others.

I think of Michael often when I look in the faces of my grandchildren. I am sure he enjoyed kissing the beautiful faces of his children as I enjoy kissing the faces of my little ones. I am sure his heart melted when they said they loved him and I am sure he would laugh as I did when my grandson said he loved me more than his Legos. When they smile at me and make me laugh I think of what they did for him to make him smile and laugh. I think of him often. When I look in their faces, I think of him.

Michael gave a speech at Oxford University to launch the initiative for "Heal the Kids" charity. "What if they grow older and resent me, and how my choices impacted their youth?" Michael asked rhetorically of his children. "Why weren't we given a normal childhood like all the other kids?" They might ask. And at that moment I pray that my children will give me the benefit of the doubt. That they will say to themselves: Our daddy did the best he could, given the unique circumstances he faced. "I hope, he concluded "that they will always focus on the positive things, on the sacrifices I willingly made for them, and not criticize the things they had to give up or the errors I've made, and will certainly continue to make in raising them. We all have been someone's child, and we know that despite the very best of plans and efforts, mistakes will always occur. That's just being human."

He was a great dad.

Michael lost so much in his life. In the end what did he have? Thank God for Debbie Rowe. Thank God for those children.

Chapter 23

Me

From the time I was nine years old special children would find me wherever I went. Once I left a library holding my children's hands only to look over and see my 3 year old daughter 3 feet from me. The child who grabbed my hand was a special child.

I had been in the profession of teaching children and adults in public schools for over twenty years. I have taught ballroom dance to severely and profoundly handicapped people and was a foster parent to a special child. I am currently retired and own my own business.

As for these types of people, I have an uncanny ability to know what they are thinking and what they are trying to say. My friend calls me discerning. I think I just see them as people and the rest falls into place.

I have to say never in my wildest dreams did I think I would be writing a book about Michael Jackson, especially, one like this.

I wondered what I would have done if in had known this information before Michael died. I know I would have had to tell him. I couldn't have let a little boy flounder in confusion. I very well may have paid a heavy price for it as I may even now, but I would have had no choice.

I would have done my best to tell him there were other Peter Pans in the world and they will give you want you need so you don't have to hang out with little boys and get in any more trouble.

Would the Handlers have tried to stop me? Maybe. Would the Gatekeepers tried to stop me? For sure. Would challenging what the public and the big bucks wanted people to think about Michael be like trying to stop a train by standing in front if it with my hand up? Probably.

I have fought all of my life for people like Michael or should I say for the purposes of this book, people I believe Michael to be. I fought big people and little people and even institutions. But never did I think I would be going against...Uh, I don't know what.

Some of the topics were easy to write because they came to me while driving or in the middle of the night. Actually, they often haunted me to be written. Others had to be researched which required that I read about Michael or hear him speak on YouTube. I have to say those times when I had to hear his voice were so hard for me and I had to wait for the right time when I was able to handle it. It often made me cry and had to be done at a time when I didn't have to be anywhere special that day.

I was haunted by what I knew and had to write it down if not to free Michael, to free myself. I was haunted every free moment I had and then one day it stopped. All the questions I had were answered. I was at peace.

Writing this book was cathartic for me. I had the time and certainly needed to clear my head. I believe this book will once and for all clear his name.

This is all I know about the Michael I met on that fateful day. I can just hope you understand my motives and that I don't go down with the ship.

Now that this book is written I am terrified of what it might bring to me. Today I stop crying and writing and maybe begin being scared.

Chapter 24

What Can We Do For Michael Now?

What you can do for Michael now...

It is my hope and my prayer that after you read this, if you were one of the people who loved Michael Jackson, you will love him still and if you were not you will love him now. After all if the tables were turned, he would have loved you.

We can't bring Michael back but there are two things we can do for him from here. First you can reject any negative thing said or written about him. They had their time. This is Michael's time now.

If you hear any jokes about Michael on the television change the channel. If you see any negative thing written about Michael in a tabloid don't buy it. You can read it if you care to but after the research I had done here I learned that most of it is made up so why waste your time.

But if you choose to read it, don't buy the paper. If you choose to read it promise yourself you will not buy the paper.

They have made enough money off Michael.

The headline in the Mirror on September 07, 2009 said, "Paris Jackson Unmasked: The weird world of Michael Jackson's daughter.

Already it's starting. Already they are writing about the children. Paris is eleven years old and her name is in the tabloids.

Michael was talking with Barbara Walters about his children and their plight.

Michael: "I want to have some space where they can go to school. I don't want them to be called Wacko Jacko.

Barbara: How are you going to prevent it?

Michael: That's the thing. That's the idea. Maybe you should come up with a plan to help me.... It's hurting my heart. Why pass it on to them?

Michael was not even buried yet when they paraded the faces of the kids he tried so desperately to hide before the entire world.

"I concealed their faces because I wanted my children protected... in public I must protect them." [64]

To the fans who say they love Michael Jackson let me say, do you love him unconditionally? Do you love him as he had loved the thousands of children of all afflictions that entered his life? Let's hope so.

Albert Einstein: He who joyfully marches to music in rank and file has already earned my contempt. He has been given a large brain by mistake, since for him the spinal cord would suffice.

Don't march in rank. Do what is right. When you hear a Michael Jackson put down or joke or when you hear accusations, remember to have the courage to defend him.

188

Have the courage.

When you want knowledge about the kids or Michael don't buy a tabloid.

If you see the children in public:

Don't say, "I loved your father's music."
Don't say, "I loved your father."
Don't say, "I am sorry for your loss."
Don't say, "Those tabloids are so mean."
Don't say, "Michael was a great guy."
Don't say, "Michael was a great father."
Don't say, "I hope you are alright."
Don't say, "How are you doing?"
Don't say, "I miss your father."
Don't say, "I listen to him all the time."
Don't say, "I like your shoes."
Don't say, "I like your shirt."
Don't say, "Can I have your autograph?"
Don't say, "I have your father's autograph."
Don't say, "My son loves your father's music.'
Don't say, "Have a good day."
Don't say, "Hey, it might rain."

DON'T... SAY... ANYTHING!

If you care about Michael at all, if you want to right some of the horrible wrongs done, if you care about him as he had cared about others, you will do this one thing for him, you will give his children the freedom he didn't have. You will do the one thing that needs to be done. You will do...

NOTHING!

Chapter 25

Who Killed Michael Jackson?

I have begun to love Michael Jackson both right brain and left. I am hoping his fans will love him both right brain and left the way his friends did, the way he would have loved you.

In the end, I find it so ironic that if this concept is correct, those who used and abused Michael for their own desires, mostly money, would really be the child molesters. And those who believed that the show was reality, those who sobbed, stayed up all night yelling his name, acted so stupidly and followed him like bunnies were the wacko ones and Michael, now making perfect sense, was the sane one. I find it comically, sadly ironic.

As for who killed Michael Jackson...

Was it the Handlers or Gatekeepers who kept the façade going?

Was it the father who would not even let his son call him Dad?

Was it the people who bought the tabloids that so trapped the little boy with judgment or lies?

Was it the so called fans who screamed his name over and over in the middle of the night and grabbed at him like a thousand hands tearing at spaghetti?

Was it the teachers who taught him all of his life and never told him he was disabled?

Was it the photographer for the tabloids who tried to take his picture in the bathroom?

Was it the photographers who had no heart and sold who their souls for money?

Was it the people who judged him rather than listen?

Was it the doctors who gave him drugs he never should have had?

Was it the politicians or drug companies who restricted drugs he needed to survive?

Was it the social workers who sat in court to protect the accusing child and not the accused child?

Was it the people who idolized him instead of seeing him as a human being?

Was it the people who hid the secrets?

Was it the people who refused to believe the truth when they could see it?

Was it the people who want to believe that the show and the icon are real?

Was it the people who stole money from him?

Was it the people who made him dance like he was a teenager at 50 years old?

Was it the crazy fans who did for themselves with no regard for his welfare?

Was it the people who told him it was ten concerts when it was fifty concerts?

Was it the people who knew why he was lonely and kept quiet for money?

Was it the people how look down at those with handicaps or who are different?

Was it the doctor who gave him the lethal drug that killed him?

the list goes on and on....

But who really killed Michael Jackson...

us

Bibliography

01. Tatiana Thumbtzen
02. Childhood by Michael Jackson
03. Michael Jackson the Man Behind The Mask
04. Private Home Movies of Michael Jackson Part 3
05. Martin Bashir: Living With Michael Jackson
06. Michael Jackson the Man Behind The Mask
07. The Michael Jackson Tapes Rabbi Shmuley The Michael Jackson Tapes by Rabbi Shmuley Boteach Pg. 135
08. Private Home Movies of Michael Jackson Part 5
09. Michael Jackson: the Man Behind The Mask
10. Google: Michael Jackson Oprah interview
11. Michael Jackson: The Music and the Madness page 168
12. Google: Michael Jackson poems
13. Neverland tape
14. http://www.youtube.com/watch?v=j4eP6Gfh5OQ
15. Wikipedia Michael jackson
16. Wikipedia Michael Jackson
17. Michael Jackson: The Music and the Madness Pg 21
18. Michael Jackson: The Music and the Madness pg 22
   19. Michael Jackson: The Music and the Madness pg 22
20. Michael Jackson: The Music and the Madness pg 35
21. Martin Bashir: Living with Michael Jackson
22. Michael Jackson The Man Behind The Mask
23. http://www.youtube.com/watch?v=pLEZToPZ2pI
24. Michael Jackson: The Music and the Madness pg153
25.http://musicians.about.com/od/interviewsandbios/p/tommymottola.htm
26. Google: Michael Jackson Interview With Barbara Walters (Part 2)
27. Michael Jackson: The Music and the Madness pg 373
28. Michael Jackson: The Music and the Madness pg 519
29. Michael Jackson: The Music and the Madness pg 144

30. Michael Jackson: The Music and the Madness pg 632
31. Michael Jackson: The Music and the Madness pg 263
32. Michael Jackson: The Music and the Madness pg 88
33. Michael Jackson: The Music and the Madness pg 100
34. Michael Jackson: The Music and the Madness pg 148
35. Michael Jackson: The Music and the Madness pg 175
36. The Michael Jackson Tapes   by Rabbi Shmuley Boteach
37. Michael Jackson: The Music and the Madness pg 256
38. http://transcripts.cnn.com/TRANSCRIPTS/0405/27/lkl.00.html
39. http://www.youtube.com/watch?v=RtgqiJnXRKg
40. http://www.youtube.com/watch?v=BhtilFuONlA
41. http://www.youtube.com/watch?v=4oN4bc52dYM&NR=1
42. http://www.thisislondon.co.uk/showbiz/article-20588589-jacko-mobbed-by-fans.do
43. http://www.gazotube.com/e5M0YTu9CC8.html
44..http://view.picapp.com/default.aspx?iid=4175232&term=michael+jackson+kids&tpid=4175232%3B6315976%3B6151278%3B6151277%3B6151276%3B6109451%3B6109446%3B6109445%3B6109444%3B6109443%3B6109441%3B6109439%3B6109437%3B6109435%3B6109434%3B6109433%3B6109431%3B6109432%3B5806144%3B5806143%3B5806141%3B5806139%3B5806138%3B5806136%3B5806132%3B5806131%3B5784232%3B5784231%3B5784230%3B5784229%3B5784228%3B5784227%3B5784226%3B5784225%3B5741990%3B5741991%3B5741992%3B5741993%3B5741994%3B5741995%3B5741996%3B5335721%3B5090565%3B5089501%3B5089354%3B5089281%3B5089252%3B4938158%3B4938155%3B4938137
45. http://www.gigwise.com/news/50643/Michael-Jackson-Mobbed-By-Fans-During-LA-Shopping-Trip
46. http://www.youtube.com/watch?v=viwHCX9dU6I&feature=related

47.http://www.metro.co.uk/fame/article.html?Michael_Jackson_mobb ed_leaving_hospital&in_article_id=480931&in_page_id=7
48.http://www.metro.co.uk/fame/article.html?Michael_Jackson_mobb ed_leaving_hospital&in_article_id=480931&in_page_id=7
49. http://news.bbc.co.uk/2/hi/entertainment/4325820.stm
50.http://www.youtube.com/watch?v=8geGu4mexgo&feature=related
51.http://transcripts.cnn.com/TRANSCRIPTS/0906/29/lkl.01.html
52. http://en.wikipedia.org/wiki/Marlon_Brando
53. http://www.myfreedompost.com/2009/06/michael-jackson-and-ronald-reagan.html
54. "Oona: Living in the Shadows" by Jane Scovell
55. Michael Jackson: The Music and the Madness pg 341
56. Michael Jackson: The Music and the Madness pg 342
57. Michael Jackson: The Music and the Madness pg 209
58. http://www.bettyconfidential.com/ar/ld/a/Autoimmune-disease-and-women.html
59.http://www.itnsource.com/shotlist//RTV/1996/09/16/609160011
60.http://entertainment.timesonline.co.uk/tol/arts_and_entertainment/music/article6586759.ece
61. http://www.youtube.com/watch?v=RtgqiJnXRKg Michael Jackson Interview With Barbara Walters (Part 2)
62. http://www.dailymail.co.uk/news/worldnews/article-1197247/Inside-Neverland-The-stunning-photographs-Michael-Jacksons-fantasy.html
63. Michael Jackson: The Music and the Madness pg 636
64. Michael Jackson: The Music and the Madness pg 525
65. Michael Jackson: The Music and the Madness pg 637

Please take the time to go to YouTube and watch: The Michael Jackson The Footage You Were Never Meant To See and for a cute Michael see the interview with Barbara Walters.

I would like to express my thanks to Mr. Tamborelli and YouTube for the bulk of the details for this book.

Made in the USA
Lexington, KY
05 March 2010